ep EP Publishing Limited
1977

Blacksmith at Bradfield, Berkshire (*Univ. Reading, M.E.R.L.*)

EXPLORING COUNTRY CRAFTS

J. GERAINT JENKINS

ABOUT THE AUTHOR

John Geraint Jenkins, M.A., F.S.A. is a native of Llangrannog, Dyfed, and is now on the staff of the Welsh Folk Museum where he is Keeper of Material Collections. He was previously on the staff of the Museum of English Rural Life, University of Reading. He is Editor of the journal *Folk Life* and Chairman of the Society for the Interpretation of Britain's Heritage. From 1968 to 1973 he was Recorder of the Anthropological Section of the British Association for the Advancement of Science. He has published a number of books, amongst them being: *The Welsh Woollen Industry*, *The English Farm Wagon*, *Agricultural Transport in Wales*, *Nets and Coracles*, *Traditional Country Craftsmen* and *Life and Tradition in Rural Wales*. He is married with three children and his first language is Welsh.

The cover photograph was taken in the Wheelwright's Shop, Shibden Hall, Halifax—Calderdale Museums service.

ISBN 0 7158 0469 3

Published by EP Publishing Ltd, East Ardsley, Wakefield, West Yorkshire, 1977

Text set in 10/11 pt Monophoto Univers, printed by photo-lithography, and bound in Great Britain by Butler & Tanner Ltd, Frome and London

CONTENTS

INTRODUCTION

Until recent times, every region in Britain possessed its own character and personality and it is only within the last fifty years or so that much of that personality has been eroded with the spread of standardisation in both material and non-material things. These great standardising influences have tended to make all parts of the country similar in outlook and sense of values, for no longer does the countryman look towards his own village or locality for the means of life. Today, the products of the industrial districts are within reach of even the remotest farmhouse in the hills; the newspapers and television are constantly encouraging the countryman to buy goods and articles that are exactly the same in all quarters of the globe. The character of community life is becoming so standardised that the various regions of Britain are rapidly losing their identity.

Until recent times each locality in Britain had its own range of agricultural tools, of ploughs, shovels, carts and wagons; each locality had its own distinctive architecture, its own dialect variation and its own peculiar brand of social organisation, custom and spiritual culture. Just as the features of an individual—complexion, colour of hair, accent, voice and many other features—all add up to give that individual's personality, so too do the features of a region—the cultural landscape, architecture, dialects and numerous other elements—all add up to give that region's personality.

Undoubtedly the country craftsman contributed in no small measure to the personality of regions in Britain, and everywhere in the landscape may be seen evidence of all the activities of past generations of country craftsmen. Many of them worked in a tradition that went back for hundreds of years; a tradition that varied tremendously from one region to the other. Take, for example, the work of country builders in Wales. The traditional houses of Wales, as elsewhere, owe their design and layout to a complex interaction of geological, geographic, economic and social factors. The nature of the climate, the conditions of local geology and the availability of suitable building materials have all had their effect on determining the type of house found in a particular area. In the past, the countryman built his house from the materials that occurred locally; he often designed his own house; he built it according to his needs and he considered primarily, not architectural beauty of design, but the utility of the building. In so doing, country builders hardly ever followed a particular universal style or fashion that was prevalent in other regions at the time. In the Llŷn peninsula in North Wales, for example, much of the surface of the land is covered with coarse boulder clay and there is very little suitable building stone. From time immemorial, therefore, the peasant farmers of that region utilised earth intermixed with straw, cow dung and other commodities for the construction of their cottage homes. Wales is of course dominated by a high moorland plateau, dissected by deep river valleys that branch out from that central core. Along the broad valleys that run eastwards—the Dee, the Severn and the Wye—many alien influences entered the Principality. Along the valleys, for example, came the English four-wheeled wagon, the English short-handled spade and the English language. Along these valleys too came the tradition of timber-framed black and white houses in a valley region where the oak tree predominates. The standard of carpentry in those valley regions was always far superior to that found in other parts of Wales.

Just as the valleys of the Severn, Wye and Dee lead into the heart of Wales, so too does the southern coastal plain: the Vale of Glamorgan acts as a routeway from which came influences of the English Plain. Here the wheelwright's art, expressing itself in the most elegant of four-wheeled vehicles, reached a very high level of achievement. Here too was found a technique of thatching far superior to that found in any other part of Wales. Here in a vale of trim, whitewashed villages, one sees a settlement pattern and a style of building craftsmanship far more closely related to the West of England than to moorland Wales.

There are of course many other regional and subregional styles of vernacular buildings in Wales. There are the massive houses of Bardsey and St David's Head in Dyfed, with the thick walls and deeply recessed windows which befitted districts where the force of westerly gales blowing in from the sea could easily destroy more fragile structures. There are the stone cottages of Snowdonia, a land of dry-stone walls, of slate roofs and massive boulders, constructed by past generations of craftsmen who worked and understood stone. But much of Wales consists of a vast moorland plateau of scattered homesteads, with many of the dwellings located on a windswept upland where it was important to have access to cattle at all times. For this reason, the longhouse that accommodated man and beast under the same roof became commonplace in Wales. In the building of houses, craftsmen followed a tradition and built their structures according to both needs and conditions. This was a characteristic of all country craftsmen, for in other spheres, such as making tools and implements for the farming population of their own localities, they took into full consideration such features as soil and vegetation as well as the ingrained traditions of their localities.

Take, for example, the work of country wheelwrights; craftsmen who in their way became artists as important as those who applied paint to canvas. They were asked to make the simple things, the utilitarian things that the rural community required; they were asked to build vehicles that were expected to last for a a long time. But in the wake of this utilitarian purpose, there followed pride in creating something useful and durable, but creating it with beauty and good taste. Take, for example, the Cotswold wagon, described by Marshall in 1788 as 'beyond all doubt the best I have seen in the kingdom'. Not only was this vehicle one of great beauty but it was also well suited to the topography and economy of the Cotswold countryside. Generations of wheelwrights in such places as Lechlade and Eastleach, Burford and Stow-in-the-Wold built their wagons as light as possible, cutting away excess weight as befitted an area that had many changes of slope. The narrow-wheeled wagons that were always painted in a delicate shade of yellow were equipped with waisted sides for easy turning in fields and narrow lanes; and since the economy of the Cotswolds was traditionally based on sheep rearing and cereal cultivation, the wagons were equipped with nearly horizontal end-ladders and side-boards to take loads of corn sheaves. The tradition of the Vale of Berkeley between the Cotswolds and the Severn was entirely different, for here on heavy clay, local wheelwrights in Oldbury and Shepperdine, Sharpness and Thornbury equipped their heavy blue-coloured vehicles with broad wheels that would not sink into the clay. The Vale was pasture land, and since hay was the main farm crop the wagons were equipped with wide and solid overhanging side-boards with nearly upright end-ladders to take heavy loads of loose hay. Since the lanes of the Vale of Berkeley are straight and often built on embankments above the flood plain, the locking capabilities of wagons was not a prime consideration. In every region of Britain, agricultural vehicles and indeed anything else required by the countryman were well suited to the environment for which it was designed.

By far the most widespread of rural crafts were those where the craftsman was concerned with supplying local needs. Those were the craftsmen who were essential to the life of every rural community and who looked no farther than the inhabitants of a particular district for their market. Craftsmen such as saddlers, wheelwrights, blacksmiths, coopers, carpenters and many others were in this category and it is the craftsmen belonging to this particular class who have disappeared more than any other. Today most of the countryman's needs are met by national or even international organisations and the advent of mass production, mass advertising and mass transport have meant the death of numerous crafts that were dependent on a local market. A Hereford village in 1900, for example, had a corn miller, a maltster, three carpenters and joiners, a wheelwright, a blacksmith and a cooper. Today it has no craft workshops. Crickhowell, a Brecknockshire market town, had in 1830 three joiners, a saddler, two tailors, two hatters, three boot makers and two blacksmiths. It had two maltsters, two masons, a wheelwright and a tiler. Today Crickhowell has few craftsmen concerned with supplying a local market.

The great changes in rural life have come into being since the end of the First World War and those changes have been greatly accelerated since 1945. No longer does the countryman look towards his own locality for the means of life. The craftsman has lost his place as an essential member of the rural village

or neighbourhood and his contribution to the variety of country life has been replaced by a monotonous standardisation so characteristic of the last quarter of the twentieth century. Those who remain at work are vestiges of a past era when the community looked no farther than its own boundaries for the essentials of daily life.

Many of the creative craftsmen of the past whose successors still practise a trade are now principally service craftsmen responsible for the repair and renovation of farm and domestic equipment. The joiner is concerned with building repair and maintenance; the cobbler is a repairer rather than a maker of boots and shoes, while the blacksmith is in most cases an agricultural engineer concerned with the repair of factory-made farm equipment. Indeed the great changes of the last fifty years have affected the blacksmith more than any other craftsman, for today, with the exception of those who are concerned with making wrought-iron work, most are service workers. In the past, when the horse provided the only motive power on the farm and the equipment and machinery of agriculture remained simple, the blacksmith was a creative craftsman, essential to every rural community, responsible not only for repairing but also for making a wide range of farm and domestic equipment.

The types of rural craft that have persisted to a greater extent are those that came into being because of the presence of a raw material in a particular location. Basket makers still flourish in central Somerset, for example, because of the availability of willow on the flat, marshy moors of the district. The slow, meandering River Parrett often bursts its banks and floods hundreds of acres every winter. Basket willow thrives on thick, loamy soil, on land that is sometimes flooded, but at other times well drained, and due to the ideal conditions for the growth of willow, basket making flourishes in Sedgemoor. The availability of sycamore in the Teifi valley in West Wales was the reason why bowl making became important in such villages as Aber-cuch and Henllan, while the besom makers of north Hampshire depend on the ample supply of birch that grows so profusely in the region. Indeed when one looks at modern industry such as the furniture industry, its location in High Wycombe is in no small measure due to the craftsmen that once practised their trade in the beech woods of Buckinghamshire. Country craftsmen were essential members of every rural community, for in the past most country people realised their ambitions within their own communities; they were born, they lived and they died within the confines of their own localities, to which they were tied by ties of blood, family and neighbourliness. Most of the food required by the community could be produced locally: the countryman had animals that could supply him with meat, milk, skins and wool. He had fields, gardens and orchards that supplied him with cereals, root crops, fruit and vegetables. Until the mid-nineteenth century at least, and even later in some parts of the country, farming depended very largely on a large labour force and on a wide range of hand tools produced by the numerous craftsmen who lived in each locality. Until recent times such tasks as baking bread, making butter and cheese, brewing beer and making cider were very much a part of the daily routine of many farming families. Pigs were killed and salted and many of the products of the farm—corn, wool and animal skins—could be taken to a nearby mill for processing. The products of those mills—flour, oatmeal and blankets, for example—could be used directly in the home, while others such as cloth, tweeds and leather could be used by another local craftsman to make some essential. These craftsmen were responsible for making the everyday essentials of life—farm tools and implements, furniture, utensils for the kitchen and dairy, horse harness, wearing apparel, boots, clogs, indeed everything the countryman required, could be produced locally. But even if a locality did not possess all the craftsmen considered essential to live, then there were always the travelling craftsmen—travelling blacksmiths, saddlers, dressmakers—who could pay periodic visits even to the remotest farmhouse.

Things have changed, for no longer is the country craftsman the essential member of the community that he once was. But even so, in the heart of the countryside today there are representatives of ancient traditions, still practising the trade of their forefathers. Many still employ the same techniques of manufacture and the same tools that have been known for centuries. For example, in the craft of barrel making, the modern cooper uses tools that are not dissimilar to those used by craftsmen in Roman times. Their technique of bevelling oak staves, of bending and steaming, of trussing and hooping has not changed in two thousand years. Again the technique of basket making has not changed from the dawn of civilisation; the technique of making wooden wheels in the twentieth century was well known to the Iron Age inhabitants of Western Europe. Yet even today, in this age of mass production, there are craftsmen turning out by hand objects of such quality that no machine can equal. Today, handmade furniture, handmade boots and even handmade bricks are greatly valued, and as in medieval times, there is a premium on skilful hands and a price on the ability of ordinary men to supply ordinary items.

WOODWORKERS

The number of craftsmen engaged in some aspect of woodworking in the past ran into many thousands. Some, like the coopers, were highly specialised; others, such as joiners and wheelwrights, spread their activity over a much wider field, producing a great variety of objects for farm and household use.

An important group of woodworkers were the itinerant craftsmen who possessed no permanent workshop. The tradition of itinerant woodland craftsmanship is a dying one, for today only a few workers practise a trade that is essentially seasonal in the solitude of a coppice or glade. It survived in isolated pockets of woodland until recent times, and the Chilterns, Furness, the Weald and Wyre Forest were particularly well known as the haunts of the picturesque workers. It survived in those trades where there is a great deal of wastage of raw materials, as in clog making, wattle-hurdle weaving and chair-leg making. It survived too in those crafts, such as charcoal burning and hoop shaving, where the finished product is considerably lighter than the raw material—a vital factor where many rural workers obtain their materials from isolated forests and glades. 'Bodging' has survived too in those trades where the tools and equipment of a craft are few in number and easily transportable. A thatching-spar maker, for example, needs nothing more than a billhook to complete his work.

A number of well-known crafts, such as birch-besom making in Hampshire, spale-basket making in the Wyre Forest and chair-leg making in the Chilterns, were in the past important itinerant crafts. In more recent times the tradition of bodging in those trades gave place to working in permanent workshops, usually in a village. There are other crafts, such as wattle-hurdle weaving, that in some parts of the country are carried out in the woodland, while in others they are carried out in village workshops.

Only a few itinerant crafts have persisted, the most notable being thatching-spar making and wattle-hurdle weaving. Some, like chair bodging, have become extinct within the last twenty years, while others, like clog-sole making, became extinct in the nineteen-forties. Some woodland crafts, like bundling hazel for drainage purposes and making spile and wire fencing, are relatively simple and demand the minimum of skill in the use of hand tools. Others, like hoop-shaving, demanded considerable knowledge of raw materials and dexterity in the use of hand tools. Some of the products, like chair legs and tent pegs, could be made very quickly by skilled craftsmen; others, like wattle hurdles, demanded hours of work, a thorough understanding of the materials, skill in the use of hand tools, together with a good eye and judgment.

In the past, a wide range of products were made by itinerant craftsmen. In the case of many of the crafts, the traditional products produced have been replaced by more modern materials. The virtual extinction of 'dry coopering' has meant the disappearance of hoop shavers, while the virtual disappearance of the clog as a piece of footwear has meant the extinction of the travelling clog-sole maker. In other crafts, such as chair bodging, factory materials and modern machinery have replaced traditional techniques with the result that all the men engaged in the trades a few years ago have been forced to give up work.

The most important group of craftsmen were, of course, those who operated in permanent workshops and were either concerned with meeting a local demand or took advantage of the presence of raw materials in a locality. Handicrafts such as the carving of love spoons and shepherds' crooks were and are still practised by individual craftsmen, many of whom do not possess permanent workshops; they may carry out their work in a farm or cottage kitchen, often as a leisure activity.

Felled timber has limited uses in craftsmanship, for the naturally round shape of logs make them unsuitable for most tasks. Timber has to be converted in a variety of ways before it can be used by craftsmen. By far the most common method of conversion is, of course, planking, and many craftsmen use planked timber as their raw material. Today, planks are produced with power-saws and may be bought, ready-made by craftsmen from a saw-mill or timber merchant, but until about fifty years ago the most common method of converting baulks of wood into planks was the pit saw. These long, two-handled saws were operated by two men—the top sawyer and the bottom sawyer—who were often itinerant craftsmen who travelled from one part of the country to the other, carrying their saws with them. A baulk of timber was first trimmed usually with a side-axe and then placed on the framework of a six-foot-deep saw pit. The top sawyer would stand on the log, while the bottom sawyer held the other handle of the saw in the pit below. Pit sawing was regarded as very strenuous work, and although the sawyers were concerned principally with converting large baulks of timber, they did undertake some lighter work such as cutting out wheel felloes, shaping cart shafts and timber for water and windmills. The top sawyer was always the senior member of the team and it was his task to mark out the logs and it was his responsibility to sharpen the saws. The bottom sawyer, on the other hand, was responsible for cutting away the bark and hewing the edge of each log, so that they could be laid firmly on the top of the pit.

The hewing of timber with a side-axe, a tool with a broad blade sharpened on one side only, is a disappearing skill, but most of the oak in timber-framed dwellings was prepared in this way. The adze, with its blade set at right angles to the handle, was another tool used for hewing solid timber, as in making the ribs of a boat, butchers' trays, wheel felloes and dug-out canoes. Adzing was until recently carried out by Chiltern chair makers for preparing the seats of Windsor chairs. The specialised craftsman concerned with this task was known as 'a bottomer' and it was his responsibility to shape the elm seats produced by the benchmen of Buckinghamshire. The seat blank was placed on the floor and held firmly in place with both feet. The blank was then quickly reduced to the correct shape with a quick chopping motion of the adze, at right angles to the run of the grain. Modern routing machines now carry out the work, and the ancient adze, so vital in the chair-making industry, is now obsolete.

To obtain broad, flat pieces of wood from a round log as in trug and spale-basket making, gate-hurdle making and coracle making, the woodworker usually resorts to cleaving. With an axe, strips of thin wood can be obtained by cleaving along the grain of a log, and to produce even finer strips, an L-shaped axe known as a frow or dill-axe is used. Some woodland craftsmen, like wattle-hurdle makers and thatching-spar makers, undertake cleaving with a billhook. The great advantage of cleaving over other methods of breaking up timber is that the craftsman is able to obtain strong pieces of wood with an unbroken grain. Many craftsmen finally shape cleft timber by shaving with a draw knife—a simple two-handed knife used by clamping the timber to be shaved in the jaws of a shaving horse. Chiltern chair bodgers, coopers, wheelwrights and coracle makers all used the draw knife extensively.

Some craftsmen, such as wattle-hurdle weavers, are concerned with plaiting thin strands of wood, while others, like scythe-handle makers and rake makers, had to make solid pieces of wood pliant, by steaming, boiling or heating. Wood-carving, turning on a lathe and the application of thin layers of veneer to timber are all methods of converting trees into a finished product, but an important group of wood-crafts in the past involved the actual chemical conversion of timber into another product. Naphtha oil, turpentine and charcoal were all produced by woodland craftsmen, and while the old country tanneries flourished, oak-bark extraction was an extensive occupation in the oak woodlands of Britain.

Every type of tree has its characteristics. For example, alder is tough and light and can withstand water. Thus it can be used for such items as clog soles and oars. Sycamore on the other hand is regarded as a first-class turning wood that can be immersed in water at frequent intervals. Since it does not taint food in any way, it was traditionally used for making dairy utensils. But even in a single tree there are variations of grain and quality, and variations may occur in one species according to soil and climatic conditions. Trees are usually felled in winter when there is no sap in the wood, for the presence of sap will cause the timber to warp, become stained and be subject to decay and dry rot, especially in enclosed places. Seasoning is therefore very important; the old country wheelwrights, for example, believed that a piece of timber should be seasoned at the rate of one year for every inch of thickness. Thus a piece of elm designed for a large fifteen-inch wagon wheel should be seasoned for as long as fifteen years. The process could be hastened by the less scrupulous by allowing the elm butt to stand in a stream for some days before seasoning.

Timbers

The principal timbers used by country craftsmen in Britain are the following:

Oak This was by far the most important timber used by country craftsmen before about 1850. It is tough, compact and hard, and its resistance to natural decay made it the most valuable of all constructional timbers. The beauty of its grain and durability made it an excellent timber for furniture and wood carving. This, the most durable of all natural hardwoods, was used in shipbuilding, building construction, furniture making, wood carving, bowl turning, spale basketry, wet coopering, wheelwrighting (especially for spokes and hubs) and a number of the crafts where durability was essential.

Alder A riverside tree which produces timber that is light and tough and can withstand water. Being a soft timber it was used by bowl turners to produce poor-quality bowls and platters. It was also an important timber in charcoal making while alder logs buried in peat bogs for centuries produced the so-called 'Scots mahogany' that was greatly prized in the furniture industry. A certain amount of bark was used for tanning, and because of the timber's softness it was a favourite timber of hat-block makers. Clog-sole cutters also used alder as their principal raw material.

Ash A tough and elastic tree found in all parts of Britain. It is light and easy to cleave and bend. It was widely used by coachbuilders and wheelwrights, musical instrument makers, tool-handle makers, scythe-handle and rake makers and for horse harness. Much is still used in furniture making and ladder making, while the strong truss hoops required by coopers for shaping casks were produced by itinerant ash workers.

Beech A hard, inelastic timber used for many common items of furniture and turned wooden vessels but principally for chair legs. Tent pegs, shoemaker's lasts, the wooden bases of saddles and brush backs are made of beech, but although the timber is hard and strong it soon rots if it is exposed to the weather.

Birch A poor, easily bent timber used for making such things as herring barrels, bobbins and spools in weaving mills and also as a chemical reagent in copper refining. Birch twigs are still widely used in besom making.

Chestnut A strong and durable timber, but the trunk is often marred by splits, so that it is difficult to obtain large planks and beams. Used for fencing, railway sleepers and in furniture making. Hop poles and walking sticks are often made from this timber, and toys and small turned articles are often made of the horse chestnut.

Elm A very tough and inelastic timber that will withstand water. It rarely grows in forests and plantations, and it has always been widely used by country craftsmen to produce durable articles. Among its many uses are wheel hubs, ships' planks, pulley blocks, metal-rimmed athletic discuses and building foundations. It is said that elm rather than oak was the true backbone of wooden battleships, especially for those parts below the water line. It is still used for the keels of boats and for rings of wood for trawl nets, and an important use in the past was for making water pumps and pipes; the boring of elm pipes with an auger was a highly skilled task.

Hazel An important wood for making wattle fences, pottery crates, salmon traps, thatching spars, sheep-feeding cages, walking sticks, Welsh potato baskets, hoops for dry casks, scythe cradles and also for binding straw rolls as in bee skeps and 'beehive' furniture.

Sycamore A well-grained, fairly hard tree that occurs widely as animal shelter belts, especially in Wales. It is one of the few trees that can withstand the force of salt-laden winds. It is a good turning wood and can be immersed in water without cracking or warping. It possesses a pale, lustrous colour with no marked figure or pattern and it will absorb dye without the natural grain being obscured. It is widely used by 'white' coopers for making dairy utensils, by bowl turners, spoon carvers and clog makers as well as in general carpentry.

Cherry Fine grained, easily worked and polished and is favoured by some bowl turners for making decorative woodware and for furniture.

Willow A tough, elastic and durable timber. It is light and can easily be cleft into strips. It is widely used for making baskets, cricket bats, rakes, scythe handles, trugs, clog soles, clothes pegs and gate hurdles.

Lime A soft timber used in turnery and especially in making hat blocks and for making cutting benches that will not damage knives in a saddler's or cobbler's shop.

Hornbeam A very tough wood, widely used for making pulley blocks, cogs for mill wheels and for skittles and skittle balls, golf-club heads, piano keys, plane stocks and other objects where hardness and durability are essential. It is of course a very difficult timber to work, as it soon blunts tools.

Poplar A soft and pale wood resistant to wear and splintering. It was widely used for the floor of carts and wagons and for other tasks where cutting down weight was desirable.

Those crafts which employ coniferous trees are less well developed in Britain than on the European continent, although immigrant species of conifer are widely used in the building industry. Imported hardwoods—teak and mahogany, for example—are also extensively used, especially for furniture making.

TRAVELLING WOODWORKERS

A chair bodger's hut in the beech woods near High Wycombe, 1954 (*Univ. Reading, M.E.R.L.*)

The tradition of itinerant craftsmanship has virtually disappeared within the last ten years although a few charcoal burners, wattle weavers and oak-bark extractors may still be found in some parts of the country. Before 1939 underwood crafts were commonplace, and bodgers who set up workshops in isolated forest glades were to be found in almost every well-wooded part of England and Wales.

Chair Bodging

This was the best known of all itinerant crafts and it was carried out by craftsmen in the beech woods of Buckinghamshire and Oxfordshire. The bodgers were concerned only with producing the turned parts of Windsor chairs, which they sent to the furniture factories of High Wycombe. In 1960, with the death of the last of the chair bodgers, a tradition of hundreds of years died, for no one practises this trade now in the Chiltern beech forests. The bodgers, who turned the timber while it was still green, used primitive pole lathes to carry out their work. 'The bodging was formerly done in a thatched hut,' said G.L. Dean, a member of a well-known Chiltern bodging family.

'This was simple to construct and very efficient for its need. Two fairly straight saplings were chosen; not too heavy and cut into twelve-feet lengths and split down the heart. The top was joined by boring a hole about ten inches from the end, through

'A hedgehog' of chair legs in Hampden Wood, Buckinghamshire (*Univ. Reading, M.E.R.L.*)

which a tapered peg was inserted and tapped tight. These formed the two ends and were opened out about twelve feet at the bottom and braced three feet from the ground with driven-in posts which were nailed in position. These were erected at suitable distances to allow for the lathe and pole and shaving horse. Across the top and resting in forks a cross bar was placed. Side rails nailed on half way up the corresponding ends and a middle piece on either side rested on the bar and under the side rail. The whole formed a framework that rested on

four thatched bundles to within four feet of the ground. After work had been in progress and enough waste about, walls were built, leaving a front entrance. The whole process of moving to a new site was completed in a day. The lathe was tried by turning out one Windsor chair leg.'

The bodgers regarded the pole for a lathe as very important, and great care was taken in choosing a young larch tree grown in a plantation of the right height and thickness. This was carefully peeled and

Owen Dean, the last of the Chiltern chair bodgers, at work on his pole lathe, 1956 (*Univ. Reading, M.E.R.L.*)

allowed to season in the open air for a year before fixing. 'The life of a bodger was a strangely enjoyable life, carefree but a bit lonesome,' said G. L. Dean. 'It was a problem in winter getting enough work prepared outside by daylight, before the evening lighting up. After dark we worked by candlelight and on the whole the huts were very pleasant to work in. The job was healthy one, though in the winter one had to be a bit tough.'

The bodgers used beech exclusively for their work, and this is a timber that can be turned whilst still green. It can be dried without warping, for it merely shrinks and produces the characteristic oval form of Windsor chair legs and stretchers. Owen Dean, the last of the Chiltern chair bodgers, could produce anything up to fifteen gross of chair legs and stretchers in a single week.

A comprehensive exhibition of chair-bodging equipment may be seen at the High Wycombe Museum.

Oak-Bark Extraction

By far the most common method of leather tanning in Britain in post-medieval times was vegetable tanning. Tannin is present in a wide range of vegetable matter, but the most common source was oak bark, obtained preferably from twenty-five to thirty year old coppice oak. This was ground in a water- or horse-driven mill, working on the same principle as a huge coffee grinder, and the ground bark was mixed with cold water. This was allowed to stand in leaching pits for some weeks, before it was ready to be used as tanning liquor. The coppicing of oak trees was a very expensive process and vast quantities of oak bark were required by every tannery. Some eighteenth-century farmers regarded the production of oak bark as an essential part of the farm economy and the demand for good-quality bark was very large indeed, for the heavy leather tanneries supplying the saddlery and boot-making trades in particular were to be found in almost every district. In more recent times, oak bark

Oak bark drying in the Forest of Dean, 1971 (*Welsh Folk Museum*)

Bark mill at the Rhaeadr Tannery, Powys, now at the Welsh Folk Museum (*Welsh Folk Museum*)

was obtained as a by-product of felled trees, the method of barking adopted by the Forestry Commission in the Forest of Dean in 1973 being to strip standing oaks, leaving the trees without bark for a year before felling. The traditional method of barking was to score a tree at regular intervals of about half a yard with a barking knife. Vertical slits were then made, and semi-cylindrical plates of bark were levered off. As tannin is soluble in water the plates of bark have to be stacked in such a way that rain does not penetrate a carefully built stack. Oak bark is still harvested in the spring months in the Forest of Dean, and oak-bark tanneries may be seen at Colyton, Devon, and Grampound, Cornwall. An eighteenth-century tannery from Rhaeadr, Powys, has been re-erected at the Welsh Folk Museum, St Fagans, near Cardiff.

Charcoal Burning

Until the nineteen-fifties, charcoal was produced by itinerant burners in many of the well-wooded regions of England and Wales. The Weald of Sussex and Kent, the Wyre Forest, Furness and the Forest of Dean were particularly important as sources of charcoal. In 1952 according to a Forestry Commission Report there were 239 people concerned in charcoal burning, operating in Berkshire, Sussex, Ashford Chase in Hampshire, Devon, Montgomeryshire, Buckinghamshire, Nottinghamshire, the Forest of Dean and in Lancashire.

Charcoal burning in the Wyre Forest, 1896 (*Bewdley Museum*)

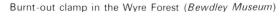

Due to the fact that the timber used by the charcoal burners is bulky and difficult to transport from the woodlands and due to the fact that charcoal is less bulky and lighter to carry, charcoal burning has always been a woodland industry. The use of charcoal is at least as old as the use of metals, and although today it is hardly used except in smelting the best-quality shear steel, it still plays an important part in modern manufacturing processes. For metal smelting it was regarded as the ideal fuel, for it produced heat that was easily controlled and was almost smokeless.

In history, it contributed very greatly to the industrialisation of Britain, for the distribution of the early iron industry depended more than anything on the sources of charcoal. Wooded valleys, such as those in South Wales, were completely denuded in an attempt to supply an ever-growing metallurgical industry with fuel. It is still used for hardening ferrous and non-ferrous metals; it is used as a filler in rubber goods, paints and plastics and as a pigment in black paint. As it is a good insulator of heat it is used in making refrigerators and vacuum flasks. It is used in sugar

Charcoal burning in modern retorts (*M.L. Wight*)

refining and, since it absorbs odours, in making deodorants. Because it absorbs colour, it is also used for refining many chemical solutions, and it still has many uses in the artificial silk industry, in medicine and horticulture.

Today, all the charcoal produced in Britain is made in metal retorts where wood is placed in a large container and a fire lit below it. The traditional method of charcoal burning was, however, the earth kiln or 'Devil's Chimney'. A smooth, level floor of earth or ash was prepared and a chimney of split logs was arranged around a central stake, about six feet high. Pieces of wood in the round were stacked around the central stake to form a large dome. The clamp was then covered with turves, earth, straw, grass and bracken; the central stake was removed to form a flue in the centre of the dome. Embers were then dropped down the flue and once alight the dome was sealed with earth. Only a small proportion of the wood in the clamp was burnt into ashes, for the secret of charcoal burning was to heat the wood under conditions where there was insufficient air for complete combustion. From two to ten days were required to complete the burning of a stack, and, by tradition, charcoal burners worked in summer and lived in roughly built shelters in close proximity to the burning clamps. Once an earth kiln had been lit and covered to prevent combustion, a twenty-four hour watch was necessary to ensure that the clamp of timber did not break out into flames.

A more advanced method of charcoal burning, a method that was still used in Sussex in the early nineteen-sixties, was the use of the potash kiln, where the earth-covered mound was replaced by a metal kiln like a huge stove pipe with a removable lid and chimney. Today, however, the limited amount of charcoal produced in Britain is produced in metal retorts, capable of holding several trunk loads of timber at a time. The term 'wood distillation plant' is used to describe the type of establishment where charcoal as well as the by-products of burning—

acetic acid, wood alcohol, tar and oils—are produced.

The old charcoal burners used a variety of timber for their work. Beech, birch, oak, alder, ash and mixed conifers were in considerable demand. Cordwood and branch wood were the main raw materials and these were used in the round without splitting. Lengths varied from eighteen inches to seven feet and diameters from one and a half inches to seven inches.

Reconstructed charcoal burners' clamps may be seen at the Weald and Downland open-air museum at Singleton, Sussex, and at the Welsh Folk Museum, St Fagans, near Cardiff.

Wattle-Hurdle Weaving

This is a craft which still flourishes in a reduced manner in the hazel groves of the chalk villages of southern England. The craft has never been very widespread and is now limited to the chalkland counties, where there is no supply of stone to make sheep folds and field boundaries. Wattle hurdles are rare in the Midlands and are unknown in the West and to the north of the Trent. In the Middle Ages when England was a great sheep-producing country, the farmers required considerable quantities of material to build fences and folds. In such areas as the Cotswolds and the Pennines, stone was plentiful and was widely used for making dry-stone walls. On the Chalk Downs of southern England, on the other hand, thousands of sheep wandered where they liked, for there was no natural timber growth and even less stone available for building fences to keep them in check. From as early as the twelfth century it became customary to enclose the most productive, low-lying part of each chalkland parish for growing coppice timber, which could be used for constructing hurdles for the downland shepherd. Because they provided shelter for the sheep, wattle hurdles rather than the gate type became popular in the southern counties. A large number of hazel coppices are still found in those counties and many still bear the name of the original planter.

The tools of a wattle-hurdle maker (*Univ. Reading, M.E.R.L.*)

A wattle-hurdle weaver at work (*C.F. Snow*)

The art of weaving split hazel in between upright 'sails' to form wattle hurdles is a craft closely related to that of basket making. Unlike the basket maker, however, the hurdle maker hardly ever works in a permanent village workshop, but from time immemorial he has followed the trade in the open air, moving his place of work season after season, as the timber supply of a particular stretch of woodland becomes exhausted. His raw material is the spring hazel that grows in coppices; that is, he uses the material growing around an already felled tree. Coppice hazel should be harvested at regular intervals of seven or eight years, for if that is not done, the hazel shoots lose their suppleness and become far too stiff for the craftsman's needs. The hurdle maker is a cleaver of wood rather than a sawyer, and the tools he uses— a billhook and cleaving knife—are for preparing supple pieces of hazel rod. The secret of the wattle weaver's craft lies in the fact that he is able to make small pieces of wood even smaller and that he uses up all kinds of hazel with little wastage. A good craftsman is able to make anything up to ten six-foot sheep hurdles on a dry summer's day.

Wattle-hurdle weavers usually buy standing hazel by the acre, or else lease a coppice for a fixed annual rent. In the past, the September auction sales of coppice wood were important events, and so keen was the demand that in many districts coppice wood was regarded as a gilt-edged security, the income from the woodland being used to endow almshouses and charities. Today, in the South of England there are extensive acreages of overgrown hazel coppices, for the craftsmen who once worked them are now few. Those who still practise the trade spend most of the year in the woodland, cutting from early October to mid-March and weaving for the remainder of the year.

The technique of making a true sheep hurdle differs slightly from that of making the plain garden type. While the latter may vary in size according to a buyer's requirements, a true sheep hurdle is always fifty-four inches long and is equipped with ten upright sails.

In addition, about twenty-four inches from the bottom, a gap is left in the weave so that the downland shepherd can stick a stake through it for carrying. Cleaving hazel rods is a highly skilled job, for the cleft rods have to be strong yet pliant enough to be twisted and woven, for a good hurdle is expected to last for many years.

Of course, wattle is not required in the quantity that it was in the past, when it was required in the construction of the walls of buildings, for ceiling laths and cart bodies. In addition there is now a limited demand from shepherds, for even that demand has declined greatly with the advent of electric fences. Wattle fences are very popular as garden fences and they are also required for such specialised purposes as strengthening the banks of meandering streams and checking the movement of sand dunes.

Thatching-Spar Making

This simple craft, which demands no tools but a spar billhook, is more often than not carried out in conjunction with another craft such as wattle-hurdle weaving. Hazel is again the most important raw material, although coppice willow is preferred in some parts of the country. It is a cleaving craft, for each length of hazel, a 'spar gadd', has to be split along its length and each piece twisted to form the spars. In addition to making the staple-shaped spars the underwood craftsmen also produced the 'spicks' or 'broaches' for pegging thatch. This included making the 'liggers', the runners fixed to the exterior of the thatch, and 'the sways', the large rods used for binding each course of thatch.

Within recent years, tarred twine, galvanised spars and metal liggers have replaced the traditional hazel spars, although in some districts the demand is still considerable.

Hoop Shaving

Hoop shavers were concerned with making wooden hoops for binding 'dry' or 'slack' barrels and also for

An itinerant hoop shaver (*Mary Hanna*)

making the truss hoops which wet coopers required for drawing the staves of a cask into shape. The craft, which died out in the nineteen-forties, was particularly common in the Wyre Forest, Furness and south Hampshire. Truss hoops for wet coopering were always of ash, but binding hoops for dry vessels could be of chestnut, willow, coppice hazel or oak.

Closely associated with hoop making was the craft of crate making for the glass and pottery industries. While the actual assembly of crates was carried out in the Potteries or near the glass works, the crate-rod makers who prepared the timber for use were itinerant craftsmen, who drew on the coppices of southern England for their raw material.

Fencing-Post Cutting

Chestnut poles of different sizes are produced by woodland craftsmen for incorporating in wire and post fences. In the woods the stakes are tied into bundles according to size and sold by the bundle to the fence maker responsible for fastening the stakes together with lengths of wire.

Clog-Sole Cutting

This was the best known of all itinerant crafts, for travelling clog-sole makers were responsible for supplying the clogging factories with wooden soles. Many clog makers in North of England towns such as Bolton and Huddersfield sent their sole cutters to the well-wooded parts of Britain, such as

Wales and the Border Counties. Some of the sole cutters settled permanently in the districts where they first came as itinerant woodmen. The tradition died out by the late nineteen-forties and the clogging factories today import most of their soles from Russia or depend on a local sole-cutting factory. Thus a well-known Huddersfield clog maker obtains his soles from a specialised sole cutter at nearby Hebden Bridge or he imports his requirements. In the past the source of raw material was the travelling clogger.

For sole making, the craftsman required a timber that did not split easily, but on the other hand it was essential that the wood was easy to shape. As clogs were widely used on farms, factory floors and mines, the soles had to be durable in water. Alder was well suited to this. It was cut in the spring and summer months, but the soles made from it had to be left to season for at least nine months before use.

Alder trees, some eighteen inches in girth, were cut into logs with cross-cut saws and sorted into four sizes—'men's', 'women's', 'children's', and 'middle's' or 'youths''. Each log was split into two, trimmed with an axe and then shaped with the guillotine-like stock knife. A deep notch was cut in the block at a point where heel and sole met and the blocks were built into conical stacks. These stacks, which remained in the open air for some months, were built in such a way that air could circulate freely between them to assist the drying process. The itinerant clogger did no more to the soles, for they were sent to the clog-making factories for final shaping and assembly.

Cutting up clog soles with a stock knife, 1939 (*M. L. Wight*)

R.B. Rigg, an itinerant clog maker, at work in the Border Counties, *c*. 1920

Thomas James of Solva, Dyfed, a village clog maker, 1969 (*Welsh Folk Museum*)

COUNTRY WHEELWRIGHTS AND COACHBUILDERS

In the fabric of community life, the craftsman working in his village workshop was essential until recent times. It was the local craftsman who was responsible for making such things as tools and equipment for the farm. Essentials ranging from field gates to horseshoes and from ploughs to shovels could be produced locally by hosts of wheelwrights, carpenters and blacksmiths. Since each craftsman was responsible for producing farm equipment specifically for his own locality, he made them to suit local conditions of soil topography and vegetation.

Of these local craftsmen, undoubtedly one of the most important was the wheelwright, responsible for producing the carts and the wagons that a community required. These vehicles were made to suit local conditions; they were expected to last a long time, but in the wake of utilitarian purposes, there followed pride in creating something useful and durable, but creating it with beauty and good taste. Take, for example, the type of four-wheeled wagon produced by generations of country wheelwrights in the Vale of Berkeley in Gloucestershire. The wagon is a very ordinary piece of farm equipment which sold for as little as twenty pounds a hundred years ago. Strictly speaking, a large box on wheels would do the work of carrying the harvest to the shelter of a farmstead perfectly efficiently, but the country wheelwright's pride of craftsmanship, the traditional workmanship

of his native region, dictated that he had to curve the side-boards over the rear wheels as gracefully as possible. It dictated that he had to paint and decorate his vehicle with bright colours, not only to keep out the rain but so that other people, perhaps in a hundred years, could say 'This was indeed craftsmanship'. Perhaps a four-wheeled farm wagon, especially those of the West of England, was a symbol of craftsmanship at its best: perfection in an ordinary piece of equipment designed for use and durability.

The general principle on which wagons were built was uniform throughout the country, despite much variation in detail. Counties and regions favoured their own particular designs, the differences being due to the varying demands of soil, topography and economy. For example, the wagons of East Anglia were heavy and box-like as befitted an area of flat land with large fields. The wagons of the Cotswolds, on the other hand, in use in an undulating region with numerous steep slopes, were much lighter, excess weight being cut down wherever possible. In Sussex, broad-wheeled vehicles were used in the clayland of the Weald, while narrow-tyred wheels were general on the lighter soils of the Downs.

In general, four-wheeled farm wagons may be divided into two types—the box wagon and the bow wagon. The box wagon has a deep, rectangular body and may be regarded as the closest relative of those wagons used on the European continent. The bow wagon, on the other hand, made by West Country wheelwrights, is quite different, for its main characteristic is the curved side-boards which curve in an arch over the large, greatly dished wheels. The shallow body and the elegant and light appearance of the bow wagon makes it a unique type of vehicle, quite different from the heavy box-like vehicles of Europe. While the box wagon occurred in eastern England, the Midlands, the Welsh Border Counties and the South-East of England, the bow wagon was limited to a region stretching from the Chilterns in the east to the Vale of Glamorgan and the Devon–Cornwall boundary in the west. It did not occur to the north of the northern edge of the Cotswolds. The remarkable uniformity that occurred in wagon design in the regions of England and Wales until the beginning of the present century was a surprising feature of country craftsmanship. Village craftsmen followed traditional methods and styles of construction, and in this way distinctly regional styles of farm wagons came into existence. The principal type and their characteristics for each area were:

Box Wagons

Lincolnshire A large spindle-sided wagon with no fixed side-boards to take the overhanging load. Used in a region stretching from the Fens in the south to the Humber in the north. Prussian blue in colour except in the west of the region where the vehicles were painted in brick red.

East Anglian The largest of all English farm wagons, used throughout East Anglia. The body is panelled and equipped with narrow side-boards to take the overhanging load. Most were painted blue, but in north Norfolk a stone colour predominated.

East Midlands A large spindle-sided wagon with railed side-boards. Occurred widely in a region that extended from Hertfordshire to the Trent. Principal colours: brown in Hertfordshire, red in the remainder of the region.

Hereford A broad-wheeled vehicle with narrow or removable side-boards or harvest frames. Usually panel-sided and painted blue. Radnor and Monmouth wagons were closely related to this type.

Worcester A panel-sided vehicle with straight body and solid side-boards. Painted yellow.

Shropshire A panel-sided vehicle with a curved profile and a deep front-board. Painted yellow. Montgomery wagons were closely related to this type.

Staffordshire A heavy, straight-sided box wagon, usually with broad double-straked wheels. Usually painted blue, but yellow predominates towards the Shropshire border.

South-East England A medium-sized box wagon considered by some as the best of all box wagons. Panel-sided body with a waist for greater lock. Solid side-boards. Painted blue in Sussex and a stone colour in Kent.

Dorset The smallest and lightest of all box wagons. Spindle sides, usually painted yellow, but blue and blue-black wagons are known.

Surrey A medium-sized box wagon, usually painted light brown or buff. Railed side-boards, panelled sides. This was the type of wagon described by George Sturt in his classic, *The Wheelwright's Shop*.

Yorkshire Small, plank-sided box wagon, painted brown. The most simply constructed of all English farm wagons.

Bow Wagons

South Midlands (Cotswolds) An elegant vehicle with excess weight cut wherever possible. Spindle-sided, waisted body and spindled side-boards. Painted yellow.

Wessex (Wiltshire and Vale of Berkeley) Panel-sided vehicle with solid side-boards, straight, unwaisted body. Painted blue.

Lincolnshire wagon of 1829 (*Univ. Reading, M.E.R.L.*)

Glamorgan Panel-sided, similar in many respects to the Wessex wagons. Painted blue.

Somerset & Devon Panel-sided body with spindled side-boards, with the arch over the rear wheels rising at the back to give the vehicle a lofty appearance. They were known as 'cock-raved wagons' in Somerset and as 'ship wagons' in Devon. The Somerset wagons were made larger than those of Devon and all were painted blue.

The craft of wheelwrighting is undoubtedly the most complex of all wood-crafts. Although in many respects it is similar to hardwood joinery, it differs in that the joiner makes his joint to fit relying on glue a great deal, whereas the wheelwright relies on tightness of joints alone to hold his work together. A glued joint would soon disintegrate where timber is subjected to constant dampness and when a moving vehicle is subject to constant jolting and shaking. So important was the quality of timber to many an English country wheelwright that he, and no one else, would supervise the felling of trees. When a load of timber was delivered to the wheelwright's yard, it was customary for the wheelwright to assign the various pieces to particular parts of carts and wagons. Thus, gently curving beech or ash was immediately reserved for making wheel felloes, straight-grained oak butts were reserved for spoke making and placed in store to season for some years before use. Naturally curving ash was reserved for making shafts, and elm for hubs. The elm, like the other timbers, had to be well seasoned and the butts were stored with the bark still on until they were thoroughly dry. Every three or four months the craftsman would visit his store to inspect the butts and any mildew appearing on the butts was brushed off with a wire brush. In some parts of the country it was customary to place sawn elm butts in a running stream, so that water replaced the natural sap in the wood, after which the drying process was hastened considerably.

Oak and ash were the main woods used by the wheelwright for building vehicle bodies. The body framework, in particular, had to be very strong and durable and a variety of techniques were adopted in making the frame. By far the simplest technique of construction was to join two parallel baulks of wood with a number of cross-pieces. The rectangular body framing is seen on all European wagons and in such English varieties as the Wiltshire, Shropshire and Dorset wagons. Many wheelwrights realised early on that the rectangular body frame, although strong and simply constructed, had one serious drawback, in that the fore-wheels soon rubbed against the frame on turning. To overcome this disadvantage, it became the custom in some districts, such as the Cotswolds and Sussex, to make the body frame in two sections, so that a waist for the wheels to turn in was produced.

For the side planks of a wagon, a variety of timber was used, but by far the most popular was ash. In some districts, especially where the wagons were waisted, it was customary to use two different types of timber in the sides. In Sussex, for example, the sharply curving front-boards were made of non-splitting poplar while the rear part was of ash. The floor of an agricultural vehicle was usually of elm and the floor could be laid either at right angles or parallel to the body frame. Whereas cross-boarding was regarded as being perfectly efficient for vehicles designed to carry hay or corn sheaves, as for example in the wagons of the Cotswolds and East Anglia, it was far from satisfactory in vehicles designed to carry other material, such as sand, gravel or manure. All these had to be shovelled out of the vehicle and the carter needed a smooth surface for his shovel to slide along. With long-boarding, the shovel would slither along the wagon floor as if the floor were greased, but with cross-boarding, an elm slat could curl up right in the path of the shovel.

Not all country wheelwrights were concerned with building four-wheeled farm wagons, for in the west and north of Britain, four-wheeled vehicles were un-

D.R. Evans of Ffostrasol, Dyfed, 1976 (*Welsh Folk Museum*)

Wheelwright's shop, Rhoshirwaen, Gwynedd, 1914

Tyring a wheel at Cardigan, Dyfed, 1975 (*Welsh Folk Museum*)

Fitting the tyre on the wooden wheel (*Welsh Folk Museum*)

Cooling the metal tyre to cause contraction (*Welsh Folk Museum*)

known and two-wheeled vehicles were used for all farm purposes. The carts of South-West England, Ireland, Wales, North of England and Scotland were varied in the extreme. There were dozens of variations in shape and design: there were *gambos*, *wains* and *trottle cars*, there were *butts*, *long carts* and *truckle carts*, but all were built by country wheelwrights whose brief was to produce vehicles that were well suited to local conditions and who followed traditions of design and construction that had existed for centuries.

Few horse-drawn agricultural vehicles are used today, but examples of the work of country wheelwrights may be seen in a number of museums. The most comprehensive collection is at the Museum of English Rural Life in the University of Reading, where examples of most of the regional types of four-wheeled wagons may be seen. Other examples may be seen at the Welsh Folk Museum, St Fagans, at Bristol, Leicester, Halifax, Huddersfield, Norwich, Plymouth, York and Beamish Museums. A collection of wagon models is on exhibition at Snowshill Manor, Broadway, Gloucester.

The building of more sophisticated horse-drawn passenger vehicles was carried out by coachbuilders, who more often than not were town craftsmen. A coachbuilder's shop would have specialised wheelwrights and body builders, coach smiths and upholsterers whose skill was usually at a very high level.

Heavy springless coaches were well known in Europe from Roman times, but it was the introduction of spring suspension in the late seventeenth century that revolutionised the craft. It developed rapidly and during the first half of the nineteenth century it reached its highest level of achievement to produce cabriolets and curricles, phaetons and barouches of considerable elegance.

The coachbuilder's work had a great deal in common with that of the wheelwright; he used many of the same tools and the same techniques of production, but, while the wheelwright was responsible for constructing a complete cart or wagon himself, the coachbuilder's work tended to become separated into a number of distinct and specialised trades. Thus a coachbuilder's workshop in nineteenth-century England could include such specialised craftsmen as body builders, undercarriage makers, wheelwrights, coach smiths, carriage trimmers and carriage painters. The materials employed in coachbuilding were numerous: various kinds of wood—ash, elm, mahogany and deal—hides, skins, hair, glass and many other raw materials.

The woods used in coachbuilding were always hard, seasoned and three-ply. Grain-crossed whitewood from North America was imported to English coachbuilding workshops during the last quarter of the nineteenth century, especially for making carriage roofs and doors. It never became really popular and most craftsmen still clung to traditional oak, elm, beech and mahogany for the construction of their elegant vehicles.

As in wheelwrighting, strength of jointing was essential in coachbuilding, but nevertheless work was on a lighter scale than that of the country wheelwright and the vehicles produced had to be brought to a much higher finish than a farm cart or wagon. Many of the coachbuilder's specialised tools were designed specifically for shaped work, for a horse-drawn carriage had few straight lines in its construction. For this reason, the timber principally used in constructing carriages was ash, a tough, fibrous wood that could be pressed into shape after boiling or steaming. One of the other qualities which made ash particularly suitable for carriage construction was the absence of elasticity, so there was little danger of warping and twisting in vehicle frames. The coachbuilder had to select his ash butts very carefully; timber grown on hillsides exposed to constant winds, for instance, would have a wrinkled appearance and be virtually impossible to plane to a smooth surface. Nevertheless, this hard wood was regarded as the toughest of all ash timbers and was greatly preferred by the craftsmen for those parts of a carriage that were not visible.

Another timber widely used by coachbuilders was elm, with its wavy, tough grain. This was used for foot-boards and seats as well as carriage hubs, and although a few carriages had elm body planks, it was regarded by the craftsmen as a difficult timber to plane smoothly. It had a further disadvantage in that the grain of the wood would show through several coats of paint. For body panels, therefore, mahogany was the most common timber used, mainly because it showed a very even surface after the application of numerous coats of paint. The Honduras mahogany was particularly suitable as this would take the curves and sweeps required for bodywork very easily. In some workshops, coarse-grained Honduras cedar was used for body panels that were to be covered with leather, but this was regarded as being far too porous to form painted surfaces. Deal was used for the flooring of carriages and for covered panels, while white boards of American pine were used for roofing.

Unlike wheelwrighting, coachbuilding was largely a town craft, and during the second half of the nineteenth century the design of vehicles gradually became standardised. The coachbuilder was able to consult textbooks and standard patterns and he even had his own periodical where dozens of designs were printed. His workshop methods, however, remained largely traditional until the internal combustion engine brought an end to the most exacting of crafts.

VILLAGE WOODWORKERS

Country carpenters—joiners, wheelwrights, coopers and tool-handle makers and many others—were essential in the past for supplying the needs of local communities throughout the land. Of these craftsmen, undoubtedly the most common are the carpenter and joiner, craftsmen usually associated with the building trade. Traditionally the carpenter is associated with work carried out on a site rather than in a workshop and he is principally concerned with fixing large timbers by nailing and pinning and with framing up, using simple joints. The joiner, on the other hand, has always been regarded as a worker concerned with fine work and, as R.A. Salaman notes: 'In the fourteenth and early fifteenth centuries, higher standards of domestic architecture were called for, and when improved tools and methods made possible the making of furniture and house fittings from smaller sections of wood, cunningly jointed together into frames, instead of the previously nailed-plank method, the art of the joiner became separated from that of the carpenter.' By the seventeenth or early eighteenth century it became usual to distinguish between the joiner, who was principally engaged in making the fittings and immovable equipment of a house, and a cabinet maker, responsible for making the movable contents. Cabinet making developed into a very highly skilled trade, and craftsmen were able to carry out work of a high calibre using a variety of timbers and the highly skilled techniques of veneering and marquetry.

Some of the woodworkers responsible for meeting a local demand still flourish in country districts although many, such as joiners and undertakers, are principally concerned with assembling factory-produced parts. The crafts which have declined greatly are those that came into existence because of the presence of a suitable raw material in a locality. Many have disappeared as mass-produced objects, often in synthetic materials, have replaced the traditional wooden objects of the past. Those wood-crafts which still flourish produce not so much the necessities of life, but its ornaments, and most flourish in areas where there is a demand for the decorative rather than the utilitarian.

Take the case of the bowl turners of rural Dyfed, who flourished in the Teifi Valley until the nineteen-thirties. The virtual disappearance of butter and cheese making in the thirties meant that the demand for craft-produced dairy ware in sycamore declined very rapidly. Butter making rapidly gave place to the sale of liquid milk from Welsh farms and cheese making disappeared. With the availability of mass-produced domestic ware in enamel, tin, china and, later, plastics, the wood turner ceased to be an essential member of the rural community. In the nineteen-thirties many of the workshops closed down and the turners who remained in the trade turned their thoughts from the traditional utilitarian necessities of the farm, kitchen and dairy, to products that had some

Carpenter's shop at Llanuwchllyn, Gwynedd, 1914

Turned ware by Gwyndaf Breese of the Welsh Folk Museum, St Fagans (*Welsh Folk Museum*)

aesthetic qualities. Timbers other than the traditional sycamore were used to an ever-increasing extent and decorative bowls in cherrywood, yew, mulberry, oak and even rosewood and teak became the main products of rural workshops. The popularity of West Wales as a tourist centre in the nineteen-sixties put new life into many a rural turnery and those craftsmen that still practise their trade in the Teifi Valley today are exclusively concerned with supplying a tourist market.

Osier-Basket Makers

This is the most widespread of all crafts and its techniques of manufacture have not changed since prehistoric times. Some of the basket makers were found in close proximity to their markets, as, for example, in West Yorkshire, where a number of basket makers in such places as Otley and Elland were concerned exclusively with making the large skips for textile mills. Basket making flourished too in close proximity to fishing ports, where the demand for a variety of fish baskets was extensive. By far the most important centres of the industry are those districts where there is a plentiful supply of willow, and Sedgemoor, central Somerset, in particular, remains the most important centre of the industry. Small villages, such as Burrowbridge, Stathe and Athelney, still provide the place of work for dozens of craftsmen, while the flat, marshy moors around the villages are extensively planted with willow.

The impression one gets of Sedgemoor is that it is an almost depressingly flat area where everything is very straight. There are the straight ditches or 'rhines' bounding square plots of land and there is a vast network of straight, minor irrigation canals. The villages themselves are ribbon-like agglomerations of houses strung out along very straight roadways, built high above the level of the surrounding land. In winter much of that land is inundated with flood water and provides the ideal conditions for the basket willow. The beds are harvested annually, and each bed may bear an annual crop of usable willow for fifty years or more. In addition to the willow beds, which every farm and smallholding possesses, there are a great number of pollard willows, fringing all the roads. Unlike the basket willow, or withy willow, which is harvested annually, pollard willow bears a heavy crop of poles, harvested only at four- or five-year intervals. They are used for the framework of the heavier type of basket, for cleft willow hurdles and the legs and framework of garden furniture.

Although in Somerset only two species of willow, 'champion rod' and 'black maul', are grown today, the basket maker uses three principal grades of raw material, each grade being known by its colour. These grades are obtained by the different treatment of the raw material after harvesting. All willow is tied into bundles, known as 'withy bed bundles', and it is all designated as 'green willow'. This is rarely used today, but in the past it was employed for making the cheaper grade of basket, wattle hurdles and for thatching farm outhouses. The main types used by basket makers are brown, buff and white willow, the different colours being obtained by subjecting green willow to a number of skilled processes. To obtain brown, the green rods are boiled for hours and then allowed to dry in the open air. In making buff willow, stripped green rods are boiled with the bark for some hours until the tannin in the bark has stained the rods to a rich golden colour. Brown and buff rods may be obtained at any period of the year, preferably after green rods have been in store for at least six months. White rods have to be obtained in the spring. Bundles of willow are placed in a few inches of water in pits especially designed for whitening. Autumn-cut withy remains in the whitening pits for six months or more, for in the spring the sap rises in the rods, the bundles are removed and the bark stripped. Pitted willow can only be stripped between the beginning of April and the middle of June while the sap is rising and the willows bursting into leaf.

Basket making is essentially a handicraft that has escaped the application of machinery, mainly because there are too many designs for mechanisation. There are hundreds of shapes and sizes of basket, but the principle of weaving varies very little. The basket maker, who usually sits on the floor with the work placed on a large plank in front of him, requires considerable dexterity to complete his work. He also requires strength, for willow, even after soaking in water, is difficult to bend and weave. Despite intense competition, basket making still remains a true handicraft that has resisted the application of machinery.

Spale-basket makers at Wyre Hill, Bewdley (*Bewdley Museum*)

A Bewdley spale maker with finished basket (*M.L.* Wight)

Spelk-Basket Makers and Truggers

Like osier-basket making, the weaving of baskets out of cleft strips of timber, known as 'spale' or 'spelk', has been carried out since prehistoric times. Although the craft hardly exists today, it was practised until recently in Furness and the Wyre Forest.

The raw material for spelk baskets was coppice-grown oak, usually twenty-five or thirty years old. The oak, which was cut into lengths of about six feet, had to be straight grained and free of knots. The pieces of oak were boiled for hours before being split into thin strips of uniform thickness throughout. By moistening each spelk in water, the craftsman was able to press the oak into shape, and as it dried out, that shape would be permanent. The tough, durable baskets, known variously as 'whiskets', 'slops' or 'swills', were used for carrying a variety of products, ranging from shellfish to coke and from animal foods to cotton waste. In addition to its strength and durability, the closeness of weave made it possible to carry nearly powdery material. Kidney-shaped seedlips were often made of oak spale in the North of England and it is said that seedlips made in this manner often outlived the more orthodox wooden ones.

Closely related to this craft is that of making 'swills' in North-East England. In the past they were often made by individual fishermen for their own use for handling fishing lines. These baskets, made of unsplit hazel, were deep at one end and gradually became shallower at the other. In use, fishing lines with hooks attached were placed in the deeper part of the swill and the baiting of each hook was done in the shallow part. Each length was covered with a layer of grass to prevent the hooks becoming entangled when casting. The swills were made of hazel rods and split cane without the use of any appliance at all. A number of hazel rods were placed on the ground and the split cane woven under and over them to form a base. At the deep end they were bent upwards and secured to an iron rim, so making the back. The sides were completed in the same way. Swills containing baited long lines were taken to the fishing grounds and cast over a tin roller while the boat was travelling.

While in the Midlands and North the closely woven spale basket was very popular until recently, the southern equivalent is the trug. This is a boat-shaped, clinker-built basket, whose shape has not changed appreciably since Thomas Smith made the first in the Sussex village of Hurstmonceaux in the early nineteenth century. The industry still continues in the Sussex village, where the descendants of Thomas Smith conduct a flourishing business. Like spale-basket making, trug making demands considerable exactitude, although Sussex trug makers have adopted mechanical techniques of splitting and shaping the laths of willow that are used for the body of the trug. Fifteen-year-old pollard willow is the basic raw material of the trugger, but the frame and handle of the basket are of ash or chestnut. The trug is exceptionally strong and durable and it is ideal for farm or garden. Not only will it withstand many years of hard and constant use, but it is also light in weight and easily repairable.

Alfred West of Aldermaston, Berkshire, a broom squire, 1959 (*Univ. Reading, M.E.R.L.*)

Broom Squires and Brush Makers

Although in the North of England besoms are made of heather, in the South birch is the timber preferred and the craft still flourishes on the sandy heathland of the Berkshire–Hampshire borders. The besom produced by craftsmen known as 'broom squires' is widely used on the farm, garden and in industry. Not only are besoms required for such tasks as sweeping leaves and in cricket fields, but they are still used in the steel industry for sweeping away impurities from newly made steel plates. In vinegar brewing too, the bottoms of vats are lined with handle-less besoms, known as 'swales', in order to filter the vinegar. The presence of birch helps to colour the vinegar and helps in the creation of acetic acid.

Winter-cut birch is the raw material required by the broom squire and this is selected from the crown of the tree. Standing birch is bought by the acre and the trees must be at least seven years old with thick, rounded crowns. The birch is cut, bundled and built into carefully built stacks which are thatched and allowed to season for some months before use. The stacks must be built in a special way, for the layers have to be open enough to allow the winds to penetrate into the heart of a stack, yet they must be solid enough to resist the penetration of rain and snow into the centre of the stack and cause rot. The bundles of brushwood are built up in layers, laid lengthways and crossways alternately, each bundle head to tail with the next. The birch is ready for use when the twigs have become very hard yet pliable and tough. As in so many other wood-crafts, seasoning is of great importance, for should the timber be used too soon, the finished besom would be brittle and of little use.

Birch heads are today tied with galvanised wire, but the traditional material was strips of willow, ash, cleft oak or cane. Ash, larch or willow are used for the handles.

Broom squires work at incredible speed. The craftsman sits astride a low bench, known as 'a broom horse', picking up handfuls of birch that are clamped in the jaws of the horse for tying.

Unlike the broom squire, the brushmaker, who is concerned with setting clusters of animal bristles or vegetable fibres in wooden stocks, is largely a town craftsman, utilising modern machinery and modern techniques of manufacture. Although the industry in its old rural form has virtually disappeared, until the nineteen-thirties it was widely practised in rural parts of Devon, Somerset and Dorset, where dozens of out-workers were concerned with bristling wooden stocks in their own homes. A very wide range of brushes are made by brush makers and a variety of timber for stocks is utilised. By far the best timber is said to be beech, which will take the strain of boring dozens of holes in its surface to take bristles. The body of most brushes is made of beech, backed by another thin veneer of beech and finally backed with any timber from ebony to pine that the craftsman fancies. In the rougher kind of brush a knot of fibres is dipped in pitch before insertion in the stock, but more expensive brushes have their stocks threaded with wire to secure the fibres.

Bowl Turners

In the past, when wooden utensils were far more widely used in the home than at present, the craft of bowl turning was very widespread. Some craftsmen specialised in the production of dairy utensils, cheese vats, cream bowls, butter prints and milking stools, while others limited their activity to producing household treen, bowls, platters, candlesticks, rolling pins and nursing stools. Any beauty of form that the products of the lathe displayed was purely coincidental to their utilitarian value, for the turner was concerned only with producing goods which were functional. The simple design of turned ware has remained unchanged for centuries, for bowls and trenchers excavated from Swiss Lake villages and Iron Age Glastonbury differ little from those produced in the twentieth century by turners in Kingscliffe, Northamptonshire, and the Kennet and Teifi valleys.

Some villages such as Bucklebury in Berkshire and Aber-cuch in Dyfed attained considerable fame as centres of the craft. At one time Bucklebury Common, with its dells and dips and maze of minor roads, was a great centre of woodland crafts. There were rake-makers, broom squires, wattle-hurdle weavers and hosts of others who drew on the profuse timber growth of the area to produce a great variety of goods for farm and household use. Some of these craftsmen worked on a part-time basis, many of them grazed horses on the common land, but most of them were employed as full-time craftsmen. One of the best known of all, not only in Bucklebury but in the whole of England, was the bowl turner George William Lailey. For nearly eighty years he practised a craft that had been in his family for well nigh on two hundred years, and the small isolated hut in the hamlet of Turner's Green was well known.

George Lailey was the eldest of eleven children and he started work with his father, himself a renowned craftsman, when he was no more than nine years of age. When his father died, George Lailey took over a flourishing family business employing a number of workers. During the 1914–18 War all the employees left him and, except for short periods, Lailey worked alone afterwards, for he failed to induce any young man to enter a trade that demanded great exactitude and long hours.

In December, 1959, George Lailey died, and with him died a tradition that went back for many hundreds of years, for he was the last of the famous Bucklebury bowl turners. During his lifetime the fame of Bucklebury had spread far and wide and hundreds of people visited the wooden hut on the common during the course of the year. Like his father before him, Lailey was not dependent on this casual trade, for a number of London stores provided a ready market for all the bowls he could produce. His tools and equipment were presented to the University of Reading's Museum of English Rural Life, where they are now housed.

Although a great variety of timber may be used in bowl turning, the Bucklebury turners always favoured elm. Elm occurs very widely on the common and there was always a plentiful supply close at hand, but it has one great advantage over other woods in that it does not split or crack very easily and, for this reason, is eminently suitable for turning. Due to its tough nature, Lailey could turn a number of bowls from a single block of wood, one bowl inside the other, with very little wastage. Neither north-country craftsmen who used poplar nor Welsh turners using sycamore could ever adopt this technique of manufacture.

In the history of Welsh wood turning, the Teifi Valley in West Wales was by far the most important centre of the industry, and the village of Aber-cuch in north Pembrokeshire was until recently a particularly important venue of woodland craftsmanship. No more than fifty years ago there were at least seven families dependent on the craft; there were others who worked on a part-time basis, combining farming or some other occupation with a certain amount of bowl turning. The fame of Aber-cuch as a centre of remarkable craftsmanship had spread far beyond the boundaries of Wales and, even in the mid-thirties, the prospects of the industry were regarded as excellent. A guide issued in 1935, for example, said 'the growing recognition of the aesthetic beauty of the well turned bowl is creating a new demand for the products of the wood-turner'. Yet by 1962 the last representative of a long line of craftsmanship was dead and it is only in recent years, as a result of the impetus given to rural crafts by the tourist trade, that wood turning has been revived in Aber-cuch. In the past, the Aber-cuch craftsmen visited all the markets and fairs of West Wales and the turner's stall was a feature of most fairs and markets in the region. Today, members of the Davies family, who were the principal turners of Aber-cuch, are still engaged in that trade; the one craftsman is concerned with producing decorative ware, the other with the manufacture of tool handles on a large scale.

Both aspects of turnery—the production of domestic requirements and the production of farm tools—have always been the concern of the Aber-cuch craftsmen. Specialisation in one aspect of the work or the other only came in the nineteen-thirties with the decline in demand for utilitarian ware. The notable brothers, John and James Davies, who later in life specialised in decorative woodware and farm tools respectively, were in their younger days concerned with producing a very wide range of turned ware.

Coopers

One of the most intricate of all wood-crafts is that of cask making, for the cooper rarely uses any written measurements or patterns to make a cask of specified girth and capacity. One of the secrets of the trade is to know the number and dimensions of the staves that are required to make a vessel of a particular size and in the accurate shaping of those staves to fit tightly together. Not only must the craftsman make his casks so that they are perfectly watertight, but he must also ensure that each one holds the exact intended contents of liquid. Each cask must be strong enough to withhold the great force of fermenting liquids; it must last for many years despite much rough handling and frequent journeys.

Coopering is a rapidly dwindling trade, for other types of containers are rapidly gaining ground and the number of craftsmen still employed in the trade is very small indeed. Not very long ago the craft was widespread, for not only did every brewery in the land possess its cooper's shop, but coopers were essential members of ships' crews, while master coopers making a great variety of products from butter churns to harvest bottles were to be found in most large towns. Today the trade is concentrated in a few large breweries, but the craftsmen spend most of their time repairing barrels which have been in circulation for many years.

In the trade, the following terms are used for the various sizes of casks:

Beer

Butt	106	gallons
Hogshead	54	gallons
Barrel	36	gallons
Kilderkin	18	gallons
Firkin	9	gallons
Pin	4½	gallons

Spirits

Butt	108–120 gallons
Port Pipe	108–112 gallons
Puncheon	80–100 gallons
Hogshead	48–56 gallons
Quarter	26–32 gallons
Octaves	20 gallons
Kegs	below 15 gallons

The only timber used in wet coopering is oak. For spirits, American oak is preferred; for wine, oak grown south of latitude 50° is used. In Britain, very little native oak is used today, and the main sources of supply are Germany, Russia and Iran. Different qualities of wood are required for different classes of work. For example, porosity is essential in some wine casks to allow for the passage of air through the wood to assist fermentation. For spirits, the wall of the cask must be so tight that neither water nor alcohol can escape, and for this reason cleft staves cleft along the radius of a tree trunk are used—the natural concentric rings of the tree making the barrel perfectly tight.

The least specialised category of the craft is dry coopering. The dry cooper is concerned with making casks to hold non-liquid substances such as flour, tobacco, sugar, apples or crockery. The work is far less exacting than wet coopering, for the staves are less tightly held together and the barrels, which are bound with ash or hazel hoops, are far less bulged. Douglas fir is mainly used for the staves, but elm, spruce, poplar, beech and number of other woods may also be used. At an early date machinery replaced hand work in the manufacture of slack barrels, and both the staves and the heads are cut into shape mechanically. The staves are arranged inside a hoop until a complete circle is formed. They are then steamed until pliable and a windlass is employed until the free ends are drawn together to the shape of a

Initiation of cooper's apprentice at a Reading Brewery, 1958 (*Univ. Reading, M.E.R.L.*)

barrel. The staves, now in the shape of a barrel, are fired or heated to set them in a barrel shape. The barrel is trussed and sometimes chamfered and crozed in much the same manner as in wet coopering. If the barrel is required to hold a powdered product, the staves are often tongued and grooved to fit into each other and afford a tight joint. This category of the craft is known as dry-tight coopering, and is a little more exacting than dry coopering but less so than wet coopering.

The second main category of the craft is white coopering, a category that disappeared almost completely in the late nineteenth and early twentieth centuries. The white cooper made pails, butter churns, washtubs and other utensils for dairy and household use. The craft was carried on almost exclusively in villages and smaller towns. The main material used by the white cooper was oak, together with a certain amount of ash and sycamore. The process of manufacturing a tub or bucket is substantially the same as

Village cooper at work in Herefordshire, c. 1930 (M. L. Wight)

Michael Harte, cooper at the Welsh Folk Museum, shaping cask stave (Welsh Folk Museum)

in wet coopering, except that in the manufacture of a tight barrel the staves are used to cut along the grain of the wood when smoothing the inside of the cask, while in white coopering the stave is used across the grain.

Many of the medieval trade gilds practised some form of initiation ceremony, which had to be undergone by apprentices at the end of their time. In coopering, the traditional ceremony is still performed whenever a craftsman ends his five-year apprenticeship.

The apprentice first of all makes a headless fifty-four gallon hogshead, as evidence that he is a qualified craftsman. With due ceremony this is rolled to the centre of the workshops, the apprentice is grabbed by a number of colleagues and lowered into the cask. Wooden truss hoops are then beaten on, followed by a red-hot iron end hoop. Soot, flour, wood shavings, water and beer are poured into the cask and on to the apprentice as he squats at the bottom. The cask is turned on its side and with the

Inserting truss hoops (*Welsh Folk Museum*)

Trussing up (*Welsh Folk Museum*)

apprentice still inside is rolled three times round the workshop floor. The young craftsman then emerges to receive his indentures from his master. Undoubtedly this ceremony is a survival from medieval times, for the ordinances of the Coopers' Company suggest that some form of ceremony had to be undergone by apprentices before the wardens of the company presented them to the Chamberlain of the City of London, as fit and proper persons, qualified to take up their freedom. Many museums have collections of coopers' tools, but a master cooper, Michael Harte, demonstrates his work daily at the Welsh Folk Museum, St Fagans, near Cardiff.

Rake Makers

The simple hand rake is a farm tool of great antiquity, and rakes produced by a few country craftsmen in Britain today differ but little from those illustrated in medieval psalters and manuscripts. Throughout the centuries, the wooden rake was considered indispensable in the hay and corn fields, but within the last forty years, with the mechanisation of the harvest, the rake has become a far less common tool.

Hand rakes vary tremendously from one part of the country to the other and there are many variations in the methods of making them. Some are short-handled, others are long-handled; most have wide heads at right angles to the handles. In some districts, such as north Glamorgan, the rakes are designed for raking hay on sloping fields and they have short heads at an angle of forty-five degrees to the handle. There is great variation, too, in the type of wood used; those of Hampshire, for example, are of tough, springy willow, while those of Mid-Wales are of ash. In other parts of the country pine, birch and alder are also used. In northern and western Britain, where hay is often made on sloping fields and is short and springy, the hay rakes are, by tradition, small and well constructed, and each one is expected to last for many years. The rakes of southern England, on the other hand, designed to cope with the lush grass growth

of the water meadows, are much larger and less strongly constructed; indeed, the southern farmer in the past rarely expected his rakes to last for more than one season's harvesting, and consequently the rakes produced in great quantities by such craftsmen as those of north Hampshire were sold at low prices.

Due to the falling demand for hay rakes, only a few craftsmen still make them, but the most notable and best-known of the rake makers is Ernest Sims of Pamber End in north Hampshire. Over two hundred years ago, this elderly craftsman's ancestor, John Sims, started business as a specialised rake and scythe-handle maker in the small hamlet of Pamber End. At that time, he was but one of a large number of village and itinerant woodworkers who drew on the profuse willow and ash coppices of the region to produce the light, long-handled Hampshire rakes. Today in an area renowned for its woodland crafts—for here there were hurdle makers, broom squires and wood turners galore—only a few still remain at work. Whereas in the early years of the present century at least a dozen craftsmen were employed in rake making between Aldermaston and Basingstoke, only the one part-time craftsman still remains at work. There in the same low, thatched building, John Sims's descendant still follows the family tradition, still using the same techniques of manufacture and many of the same tools that his ancestor used when, two hundred years ago, he established his business.

To the casual observer, the process of making a rake is a simple one, but in order to make a tool that is durable, light and strong, considerable experience and true craftsmanship are required. A good rake must be very light to prevent fatigue during harvesting, yet it must be so strong that there is no tendency for the tines to break off. The tines must not be set in the head at too sharp an angle, or the tool will not gather the hay efficiently; if the angle between the tines and the head is not sharp enough, then the tines will tend to stick to the ground and are quite likely to break off. Yet, without any written measurements and with-

Ernest Sims of Pamber End, Hampshire, shaping the tines of a hand rake (*Univ. Reading, M.E.R.L.*)

William Thomas of Llanymawddwy, Gwynedd, fixing stays to a hand rake (*Welsh Folk Museum*)

Assembling rake head (*Univ. Reading, M.E.R.L.*)

Finished hand rake (*Univ. Reading, M.E.R.L.*)

out any form of pattern the craftsman is able to make large quantities of rakes which are perfect in every detail.

The rake maker of Pamber End may be the last of a long line of craftsmen, for it is unlikely that anyone will succeed him. His is an intricate and complicated craft; the processes involved in the manufacture of a single rake are exacting and numerous. In the past, the rake maker was an essential member of rural society, making a tool that was vital in many farm processes. Perhaps he, more than any other wood-worker, is a survival from a bygone day, from a day when a village community looked no farther than its own locality for the requirements of life.

Gate Makers

In the chalk counties of southern England two types of sheep hurdle are used: the wattle type made by itinerant craftsmen from coppice hazel and the gate hurdle made by village craftsmen from coppice wil-low. In the wide, moist river valleys of southern Eng-land the willow grows profusely and the craft of gate-hurdle making, often associated with that of making sheep cribs, was once widespread. Along the banks of the slowly meandering Kennet, for example, the willow grows well, and small villages such as Tadley, Baughurst and Aldermaston supported many craftsmen, who depended on local willow for their raw material. A number of those craftsmen were engaged in trades that supplied the needs of sheep farmers on the nearby chalk downs. Among them was the gate-hurdle maker who constructed quantities of hurdles which could be used as temporary folds and as boundaries for enclosures on the open downland.

Seven-year willow is the raw material of the gate maker, and it was customary to cut the willow poles that radiated from the stool of an already felled tree at regular intervals. Lopping of willow may be repeated for many years, for although a willow trunk may be hollow and old, it continues to bear its heavy crop of poles almost indefinitely.

Gate making is a summer craft, for the winter months are spent on the river banks, cutting and sort-ing willow. Poles are cut and sorted on the river bank, and those considered suitable are transported to the village workshop. The process of constructing a hurdle must begin in the spring, while the willow is still green, pliant and easy to cleave into the uprights, rails and diagonals that make up each hurdle. It is only after the whole hurdle has been assembled that the seasoning of timber takes place.

Gate hurdles are used exclusively for folding downland sheep, but because of the falling demand for them with the widespread adoption of electric fences, the craft of gate-hurdle making is a rapidly dwindling one.

Boat Builders

Boat building was one of the most widespread of crafts and many a remote creek and quiet waterway were utilised in the past for building a variety of vessels. Ancillary industries such as anchor smithing, pulley-block making, rope making and sail making were closely associated with boat building and although many of these ancillary trades have virtually disappeared, boat building still flourishes in many parts of the country. The ever-increasing popularity of boating and yachting as a recreational activity has brought new life to many a declining boatyard, and although fibre-glass and the synthetic materials have been increasingly used in recent years, many boat-yards still adopt the same techniques of manufacture in timber that have been used since prehistoric times. Throughout the centuries, two techniques of planking a vessel have been used. In the first the planks meet edge to edge, the joints have to be caulked and the planks are fixed to the framing of the boat with iron spikes called 'trenails'. This is the technique of 'carvel' building and it has always been less popular in British boatyards than the other method of construction known as 'clinker' building. In this process the planks are overlapped and the edges are clamped together

Raymond Russell, a gate-hurdle maker in the Cotswolds (*W.T. Jones*)

with clenched metal rivets. Caulking is unnecessary and it is maintained by many that a clinker-built boat is far stronger than a carvel-built vessel.

A variety of timbers may be used in boatbuilding, and although in the past vast quantities of native oak were required, today oak is hardly ever used except for building keels. Elm is by far the most popular timber required today and the outer planks of a boat may be of wych elm, larch, cedar or mahogany. Larch, with its natural strength and durability, is particularly favoured by some boat builders for body planking.

Boat building was the one craft where power machinery did not take over from traditional methods of hand work until fairly recently; indeed, in many yards hand work still persists. Boat timbers are still drawn with chalk on the floor of a mould loft, and the moulds themselves are cut by hand from the drawing on the floor using thin strips of wood for the purpose. These are used as patterns when sawing out the timbers. Since most boatyards construct a number of boats of the same design and pattern, the wooden patterns may be used time after time.

BUILDERS

Thatchers

Since the dawn of civilisation, man has utilised the material growing around him to provide a weatherproof cover for his home and crops. Not only do the style and techniques of thatching vary tremendously from one part of the country to the other, but the material used in thatching varies according to the raw material available locally. In some parts of the country heather was utilised in the past for roofing, but in corn-growing districts, straw, especially wheat straw, has been used by many generations of craftsmen.

Straw thatch, in addition to being attractive in appearance, keeps a house warm in winter and cool in summer. Its great disadvantage is the fact that it is an expensive form of roofing and requires constant patching and complete replacement at regular intervals. By tradition the thatcher is a self-employed craftsman, and in the past most were paid by 'the square'—a section of thatch measuring ten feet by ten feet.

The oldest method of thatching is known as 'long-straw thatching', so named because the long ends of straw are visible all over the thatch face, whereas with reed thatching all the ends are driven in to provide a brush-like finish. Long-straw thatching is less common than it was due to the fact that modern harvesting machinery tends to flatten the tubular stems, so that the straw is less compact and is not waterproof.

Threshed long straw has to be prepared thoroughly before use. It has to be wetted, the craftsman has to ensure that all the straws are parallel before the bundles or 'yealms' are prepared. Each bundle is about eighteen inches in circumference. The bundles are tied with straw rope and each one is applied to the roof and tied with spars and hazel rods. The long-straw roof is distinguishable in the way the eaves and ridges are decorated with cross rods. 'The thatched roof,' says a thatcher's handbook, 'gives the impression that the roof covering as a whole has been poured over the underlying structure; it is thus given a plastic quality, enabling it to follow the irregular planes in the roof without giving rise to any sense of rupture or stress.'

Another method of thatching, using wheat straw, is known as 'combed wheat reed', 'reed straw' or 'Devon reed'. This is seen at its best in the delightful villages of Dorset and Devon. To produce this thatching material, the wheat is not threshed in the usual manner but the ears of corn are knocked out by beating sheaves over a threshing frame or passing the sheaves through a reed-combing machine. Reed thatch is far more durable than long straw, but it has the disadvantages that it is far more expensive and that applying the thatch is a much slower process. Nevertheless, a reed-thatched roof should have a life of up to fifty years.

Hendre'r-ywydd Uchaf, a thatched long-house from Clwyd at the Welsh Folk Museum (*Welsh Folk Museum*)

Thatching a cottage in the Vale of Glamorgan, 1975

Today many thatchers will only work with reed materials, which are stiffer and much more durable than ordinary threshed wheat straw. Nevertheless, in some parts of the country, notably the Midlands and the Vale of Glamorgan, threshed straw is the traditional material used for thatching and it is only in recent years that it has become less popular in those districts. At present there are about five hundred thatchers in England and Wales, most of them practising their craft south of a line drawn from Aberystwyth to the Wash, but with important thatching districts in Cleveland in North-East England. Devon has the greatest concentration of thatchers. It takes four or five years to train a thatcher, but apprentices in the trade are few. The skill of thatching often runs in families, and although a thatched roof was once regarded as a sign of poverty, it is now becoming almost a status symbol and most thatchers have a waiting list of clients.

Stone Masons

Stone masons were amongst the most important of rural workers and in those districts where stone was used for building purposes the mason was essential. Every type of stone has its own characteristics and the methods adopted for shaping them varied tremendously from one district to the other. Thus the builder in Bath stone could shape his roughly hewn blocks of stone with saws, the raw material being soft and easy to shape. But for the Cornish craftsman, using granite, the process of dressing was quite different. Heavy hammers and a series of chisels and bolsters were required to shape the blocks into manageable building stone. In some other districts, such as the foothills of Snowdonia, the local stone was so hard and difficult to work that huge boulders which were not shaped in any way were used by the masons for the construction of house walls.

The art of stone dressing is a very old one, for the Romans were well versed in the techniques of stone cutting. With their departure the skills seem to have been forgotten, although by the seventh century Cotswold stone was being worked and used for building purposes in that area. By the eleventh century stone dressing had developed phenomenally and stone was widely used, especially for ecclesiastical buildings. Nevertheless, domestic buildings in stone were relatively rare in the Middle Ages for, says R. H. G. Thompson, 'Even the houses of noblemen were built of timber, wattle, plaster and thatch. But the predominance of timber for constructional purposes in no way diminished the scale of those buildings designed to be of stone, such as castles, churches, cathedrals, city walls and a few other constructions.'

By the fourteenth century, the mason had become a vitally important craftsman, for the master mason was almost equivalent to the modern architect, not only responsible for the construction of a building but also for its design. Under each master mason worked a number of freemasons who were qualified to carve stone and many of whom displayed exquisite artistry in their work. Stone dressing and actual construction of buildings was the responsibility of the rough masons, while under them worked gangs of building labourers who were expected to carry and heave stones.

Stone masonry flourished until other building materials, principally brick, became commonplace throughout the country. Bricks were produced by an industry that ignored all regional boundaries, so that the period after 1850 in particular saw a standardisation of both building techniques and architectural design in Britain. Unlike the bricklayer, who uses uniform blocks, the stone mason deals with irregular shapes of many different sizes. There is wide variation both in dressing stone as well as in the method of arranging those stones in the walls of buildings.

In some districts stone quarrying and working still remain important occupations. Cornish granite worked at Penryn and Penzance, for example, of a bluish-grey colour, is still widely used and exported, while of the sedimentary rocks, the stone of the Cotswolds, Yorkshire and Derbyshire are most attractive. Purbeck stone which resembles marble, the creamy, soft Bath stone and the warm brown limestone of Northamptonshire and Rutland are also widely used.

Dry-Stone Wallers

In many parts of Britain, such as the Pennines, the Cotswolds and North Wales, dry-stone walls are a conspicuous element in the landscape. A hundred years ago agricultural writers were complaining that efficient dry-stone wallers were difficult to find; today they have almost disappeared completely and only a few are able to carry out the work apart from repairing existing walls. Although no mortar or cement is used in the erection of these walls, they have to be solid enough to withstand the strong force of winds and storms on exposed upland farms. The waller's art arises in his ability to work with irregular material of many sizes, for he must size up the possibility of each stone, knowing exactly whether it will fit into a particular gap. The true stone waller does not cut his raw material to size if he can possibly help it. This is particularly true in Wales and the North of England, where the native stone is hard and difficult to cleave cleanly; but in the Cotswolds, where the stone is softer, the heavy waller's hammer is often used. This is a short-handled tool which weighs some ten pounds and has two cutting edges. One edge is very sharp and is used to cut the stone, while the blunter edge is used to crack the stone to the requisite shape.

The first task in building a stone wall is to mark out its base line with pegs or string. A shallow trench is then cut and the stones are carried in heaps on both sides of the trench and as near as possible to it. A wooden frame corresponding to the exact shape of the wall to be built is inserted firmly in the ground and another with plumb bob attached some distance away from it. Lengths of string, which will act as a guide in building, are strained between the two frames, and the task of building begins by laying the foundation stones. These are the larger, more regular stones and are laid in such a way as to provide a solid basis for the wall. The width may be as much as thirty inches at the base and particular care has to be taken in laying the corner piece or 'scutcheon' at the corner of a gateway. A large, carefully dressed boulder is laid at the corner and this must be strong enough to carry the bottom hinge of the gate.

After the base has been laid, in some districts a line of tie stones—stones laid lengthways in the form of a bond—is inserted, but in others the wall is built up to half its height before the tie stones are laid. In good-quality stone walls, the raw material is laid in such a way that each stone is slightly inclined downwards from the centre. This inclination causes rain which may have found its way through the wall to be thrown off to the sides. In addition to large stones, small pebbles of irregular shape are inserted in the body of the wall to fill all spaces. The top is levelled with large, flat stones and the coping is completed by using pointed or gently rounded stones placed on edge at the top of the wall. Heavy copestones are laid at regular intervals and the thinner stones wedged between them. Finally small stones are firmly wedged in the wall with the hammer wherever room can be found for them.

Dry-stone walling is by tradition a summer craft, for the waller cannot work in wet or cold weather as handling wet stones with bare hands is difficult. In the past, farm labourers were often competent to carry out this work. It is a task that demands a different kind of skill from that of masonry, for as Stephens says, 'We suspect that many dry-stone dykes are built by ordinary masons who being accustomed to the use of lime mortar are not acquainted with the proper method of bedding down stones in a dry dyke as firmly as they should be, and are therefore unfitted to build such a dyke. A builder of dry-stone dykes should be trained to the business, and with skill will build a substantial dyke at a moderate cost which will stand erect for many years.'

Undercutting a bed of Collyweston slate (*James Walton*)

Weathering Collyweston slate (*James Walton*)

Slaters

The attractive character of domestic buildings in Britain is in no small measure due to local roofing materials and the specialised craftsmen who slated roofs. Slating is a craft that demands considerable skill in the positioning and nailing of slates, but it also demands considerable knowledge of roof geometry. Knowing exactly how to cover a roof economically, taking into account the awkward angles of dormers and valleys, needs both training and experience. Nevertheless, today the advent of other roofing materials has led to a considerable decline in the craft of slating and the virtual disappearance of quarries that produced millions of tons of slate and stone tiles.

True slates, that can be cleft into thin slates, were widely produced in such districts as Westmorland and North Wales. The latter district was particularly impor-

tant until fairly recently for the production of roofing slates which were exported from a series of sea ports such as Porthmadog, Port Dinorwic and Port Penrhyn, that had been specially constructed to deal with the export trade. The quarrying industry gave certain villages such as Penygroes and Bethesda their own particular character and personality, for the whole life of those villages was tied up to the local quarry that could employ most of the male labour of those villages. Few quarries are in production today, but something of the history of these quarries may be seen at the North Wales Quarrying Museum at Llanberis, and at the Gloddfa Ganol Mountain Centre and the Llechwedd Slate Caverns, both at Blaenau Ffestiniog, a once important slate-quarrying centre.

In the heyday of slate, huge quarries were widespread in North Wales and they provided slates that varied in colour from green to blue. They were dressed in the quarry itself by specialised 'splitters' or 'knappers'. After repeated splitting along the bedding planes, the slates were shaped ready for use. Each size of slate was known by a specific name: 'Duchesses', 'Viscountesses', 'Broad ladies', 'Narrow ladies' and other names referring to female rank.

In addition to true slates, stone tiles obtained from a variety of rocks ranging from sandstone to limestone were widely used in such districts as the Cotswolds, the Pennines and the East Midlands. Among the most important of these were:

Horsham Stone A flaggy sandstone from the Weald Clay used throughout South-East England.

Collyweston Slate Occurs in limestone from Oxfordshire to Lincolnshire, the best quality occurring in Northamptonshire and Rutland.

Stonefield Slate Occurs at the base of the limestone from Dorset to Gloucestershire and Oxfordshire. It is quarried in blocks and often split by frost action.

Elland Flags Carboniferous slates that occur in West Yorkshire, east Lancashire (Rochdale flags), Derbyshire (Wingfield flags) and north Staffordshire (Alton rock).

Rough Rim Flags Occur near Halifax and Huddersfield.

Yorkdale and Pendleside Slates These sandstone slates occur widely throughout northern England, but quarrying as in Wensleydale has always been on a small scale.

Slaters know the different qualities and sizes of slates by specific names, many of which are picturesque names handed down over the centuries. The Cheshire slater, for example, had his 'Haughattles' and 'Widetts', his 'Jenny why gettest thou' and 'Rogue why winkest thou'.

In the Cotswolds and the Pennines the old names have persisted and slates are measured with 'slat rules' or 'whippet sticks'. These have no written measurements of any kind, but the carved symbols on their surface designate a particular size of slate which will have its own specific place on the roof of a house.

Brick Makers

Clay was used for making bricks long before man had discovered how to harden it in the heat of the fire. Bricks made in ancient Egypt were sun baked, but however hard they became after exposure to the rays of the sun, they softened again in the wet, for hardened clay has the property of absorbing moisture into its particles. It was a great technological step forward therefore when, around 300 BC, the technique of firing bricks was evolved in the Middle East.

It was the Roman conquerors who first introduced the craft into Britain and during their occupation a large number of brick works were set up throughout the country. When the Romans departed, however, the art of brick making died out and did not return on any scale until the fifteenth century. There were, it is true, one or two brickyards in Suffolk as early as the thirteenth century, but the majority of brick buildings of pre-fifteenth-century date in East Anglia were built of bricks imported from the Low Countries. They were extremely expensive and were only used to build noblemen's castles, manor houses and churches. In the late fifteenth century in East Anglia and other regions where building stone was scarce and the timber of the forests was running short, the craft of brick making took root and workshops were set up wherever suitable clay occurred. Nevertheless during this early period the new building material was still limited in its use, limited to building stately homes like Mapledurham in Oxfordshire, castles like Hurstmonceaux in Sussex and colleges like Queens' in Cambridge.

It was not until the end of the seventeenth century

that bricks became the common material for building the homes of ordinary people, and it was not until then that the craft spread very quickly to all corners of Britain. In the eighteenth and early nineteenth centuries, it was a common practice for brick makers to travel around the country, visiting places where houses were required. They tested the clay of the locality, decided on its suitability for brick making and often blended and treated it. Their techniques and processes were adopted to suit the nature of the clay. In this way a vast number of small brickyards came into existence, while in addition many of the larger country estates had their own brick works.

The eighteenth century was the flourishing period of the small brickyard in Britain, for in the nineteenth century the craft, like many others, became greatly mechanised. Many of the small yards were forced to close down in the face of new competition from the large firms. In the miles of red, yellow and grey brick work of nineteenth-century industrial Britain there is a dull monotony that was completely absent from earlier work. Whereas in the factories the clay is exuded from a machine in lengthy strips and cut up into bricks by another machine, in country workshops each brick was moulded individually; each one was slightly different from the rest and so had character. The small brickyard contributed in no small measure to the architectural harmony of a region by providing building material made from the clay which occurred locally. Not until the middle of the nineteenth century were bricks of the same kind sent all over the country from the vast, highly mechanised brick works of London and the Midlands. These machine-made products certainly destroyed the old local harmony of colour and style which characterised the earlier brick buildings. Although the majority of the old rural brickyards were forced to close down, here and there one may still find a small yard in operation, clinging to

the techniques and methods of past centuries, despite competition from large-scale manufacturers. The country yards concentrate on the manufacture of sand-faced, hand-moulded bricks, of a quality that no machine can equal. Although this type of brick is three times as expensive as the machine-made variety, they are still greatly valued for wall facings.

Finished bricks vary in colour according to the quality of the clay and the degree of firing to which they are subjected. If water is present in the clay, for example, then the colour produced at a moderate heat will be red, but a much brighter, clearer red is produced from the shales of coal measures. Staffordshire bricks are red, but by longer firing at a greater heat the bricks become blue in colour. The addition of lime to the clay makes a cream-brown brick, while the presence of magnesia produces a yellow brick. For brick making, a proportion of sand is mixed with clay, but there are many parts of the country where sand and clay occur in the right consistency, and there are others where sand is found in close proximity.

Clay for making both bricks and pottery is dug in the autumn before the winter rains set in, making the clay beds impossibly waterlogged. For some four months the nearly dry clay is left in large heaps so that it experiences the mellowing influence of frost, snow and ice. During the winter months the masses are broken up and turned constantly, so that the atmosphere can penetrate in every direction. To do this the traditional clay spades are used. These spades, made of willow and shod with metal sheeting, have an advantage over metal spades in that the clay does not stick to the blade to the same extent as it does to metal. They are also much lighter, a very important point when dealing with heavy material, and since the spade is shaped from a single piece of wood there is no danger of it cracking at the joints.

COUNTRY POTTERS

One of the oldest crafts of mankind is that of making pottery, for since the dawn of civilisation wherever there was suitable clay, men used it for decorative as well as for utilitarian objects. Throughout the ages, the techniques of pottery making have not changed in any important detail and the methods adopted at modern studio potteries at the present time differ little from those employed in prehistoric times.

Potteries of old standing are always found near beds of local clay, for the difficulty of transporting such heavy and bulky material determined their site. In Wales, for example, the potteries at Ewenni near Bridgend, at Rumney near Cardiff and at Buckley in Flintshire came into existence due to the availability of clay. A second prerequisite is fuel to fire the kilns, for although today electrically fired kilns are found in almost every pottery, in the past it was an advantage for the potter to site his workshops within easy reach of coal supply. Nevertheless, the availability of coal was less important than the availability of clay. In Devon, for example, the famous Barum ware of Barnstaple was produced in a district far removed from the nearest coal deposits, as were the potteries at Poole in Dorset, at Hailsham in Sussex and at Weatheriggs in Cumberland. Although a large number of old-established potteries still exist, the new demand for handmade earthenware has led to the establishment of a vast number of studio potteries in all parts of Britain, particularly in those districts which

are centres of the tourist trade. The craft is perhaps more flourishing than it has ever been, and although many of the craftsmen produce goods of excellent quality and design, the market has also been flooded by vast quantities of inferior material.

The methods adopted by potters are simple, for the art of the potter depends on his ability to treat and shape the clay rather than on any elaborate pieces of equipment and tools. The preparation of the clay is extremely important, for it must be smooth and of the same consistency throughout. Great care must be taken in the choice of clay, too, for in some districts such as the Vale of Glamorgan, the local clay contains limestone which tends to act as a flux when the pottery is fired, and for this reason the raw material has to be washed thoroughly before it can be used. The time for digging clay and the methods of weathering and pugging have already been described in the previous section; indeed pottery can be made from the clay from any brickyard, provided that it can be made into 'slip', the name given to it when mixed with water to a creamy, smooth consistency. This is usually passed through a silk gauze, the water squeezed out leaving it stiff enough to be shaped into balls and thrown on the wheel. For heavy, large pots the clay has to be considerably stiffer than for small pots, so as to prevent them from sagging with their own weight before they are dry enough for firing.

The potter's ability as an artist and craftsman is

Throwing a pot at the Ewenni Pottery, South Wales, 1975 (*Welsh Folk Museum*)

Robert Giles of the Rumney Pottery, Cardiff, applying slip, 1977 (*Welsh Folk Museum*)

exhibited most clearly in the age-old task of throwing, for the potter must make sure that the pots are strong yet light, and he must allow for shrinkage in firing. The potter's wheel, which in itself is a very ancient piece of equipment, consists of a revolving wheel driven by foot or electric power. It must be heavy enough to revolve steadily, and to ensure that the pots are symmetrical it must balance accurately. The thrower sits on a seat fixed to the framework of the wheel, while at the top is a tray containing the pre-

pared balls of clay. After pressing or 'wedging', to get rid of air holes, the ball is thrown with considerable force on to the revolving disc. Wetting his hands at frequent intervals, the potter shapes the spinning mass into a tall cone, flattening, raising and shaping it with fingers and thumb. Gradually the wall is thinned, the height is checked with a home-made gauge and the pot is removed from the wheel with the help of a wire cutter. It is then placed on a board, ready to be taken to the drying racks. At this stage the pots are described as 'green' and after drying under artificial heat or in the open air they are trimmed with a scraper as they revolve on the potter's wheel and all the marks are removed with a wet sponge. Before they can be fired, however, they have to dry out thoroughly and evenly.

Other methods of making pots are practised in some country workshops, the most common being the semi-automatic process of jollying. It is particularly useful when large quantities of the same product are required. The jigger and jolly machine consists of a plaster cast of the inside of a pot firmly pegged to the revolving surface of the potter's wheel. A cast of the outside of the pot is made and this is carefully shaped to a metal template fixed to a movable spring arm or spreader of the machine. While the revolving plaster cast ensures the correct shape for the inside of the pot, the spreader and its template shapes the outside. Once again they have to be turned—that is, with a metal strike and wet sponge, they have to be cleaned on the potter's wheel. For objects of an irregular shape, plaster moulds are made and the casts can be used time and time again to produce objects that are exactly the same in all details.

Green pots have to be thoroughly dried, preferably under natural conditions, before they can be fired. If they contain the slightest amount of moisture, they may explode under the terrific heat of the kiln. The correct firing of pottery needs a great deal of skill, for the quality of the finished product depends as much on correct firing and keen judgment as it does on skilful throwing. The old type of kiln, which may be coal, gas or wood fired, has to be carefully filled with the saggars containing green or glazed pottery. The saggars themselves are large round or rectangular containers of coarse pottery, often made of clay and pieces of broken crockery. The heat of the kiln is raised to a very high temperature, then allowed to cool before the pots are removed.

Pottery is fired either once or twice according to the nature of the clay and the use to which the pottery is to be put. Unglazed ware and stoneware are fired once only and the products are known as 'biscuit', whilst most glazed ware has to be fired twice. The glaze is applied after the first firing and in the second firing it is fused with the body of the pot. Great care has to be taken in stacking glazed pottery in the kiln, for no two pots must touch, while in order to see what is happening inside a burning kiln removable bricks are built into the kiln wall. Within sight inside these small peep holes are placed small glazed, fireclay cones. When their tips begin to bend over, the potter knows that the glaze is fusing and that the heat must be reduced.

Country potteries are widespread in Britain today, although few of those in production depend on local raw materials. Potteries are particularly common in tourist areas, but most of those have little to do with the traditional craftsmen who shaped local clay into pots that were used by the local community. At the Gladstone Pottery Museum, near Stoke on Trent, many of the old processes of pottery manufacture may still be seen. Here there are moulding workshops that still manufacture the utilitarian and decorative products of the industry; here the traditional bottle kilns may still be seen.

METAL WORKERS AND COUNTRY SADDLERS

Blacksmiths

The great changes which have taken place in the countryside within the last half-century have affected the blacksmith more than any other rural craftsman. In the past, the blacksmith was certainly the most numerous of all country workers and the demand for the products of the smithy were heavy and extensive. Blacksmiths were responsible for making a wide variety of agricultural hand tools which were required by a local community, and since each craftsman was responsible for producing equipment for his own immediate neighbourhood, he made those tools to suit local conditions. Blacksmiths were responsible for producing a wide range of domestic equipment from cooking pots to fire grates, and the tyring of wheels on behalf of local wheelwrights was also a part of their responsibility.

Although most country blacksmiths were responsible for shoeing horses, some were more competent than others to carry out that job, and many districts had specialised shoeing smiths or farriers who limited their activity to that important task. Since Roman times, it has been a custom to equip horses with metal shoes for the protection of hooves, especially on hard surfaces. Farriery still flourishes in many parts of the country, but the farrier is someone far more than a manual worker, for his craft demands considerable knowledge of the anatomy of a horse's foot as well as the practical aspects of making and fitting iron shoes.

In addition to shoeing smiths, the other category of blacksmithing which still flourishes is that of making wrought-iron objects, often of a decorative nature. Whatever the task the smith undertakes, the techniques he adopts are essentially those which have been passed down from generation to generation over many centuries. Just as the potter moulds or models plastic clay into the shapes that he requires, so too does the blacksmith shape hot iron by causing the metal to flow and spread in the direction that he wishes. With hammer, anvil and tongs the hot metal is shaped, for when iron is red hot, it may be bent and twisted easily; when it is white hot it may be beaten into any shape, and when it is even whiter it may be welded. The wrought-iron maker depends largely on the process of bending iron to the shape that he requires, and he possesses a wide variety of tools to carry out this work. Those tools, and indeed most of the tools required by the blacksmith, are made by the craftsman himself. The tongs seen by the dozen in any country smithy were probably made in that smithy and each one was specifically made by the smith for a particular purpose.

There has been a sharp decline in the number of blacksmiths in the countryside, for most of the tools and utensils that the smith produced in the past are now produced by large-scale industry. Not long ago no community could exist without its black-smith, but since 1939, in particular, the whole face of agriculture has changed; the tractor has almost completely replaced the horse, so that the demand for shoeing heavy draught horses has dwindled. Machinery for ploughing and cultivating the land has become more and more complex and there is no longer a demand for the ploughs and harrows, cultivators and billhooks that once emanated from every country smithy. Metal-shod cart and wagon wheels are a thing of the past and the blacksmith found that his traditional agricultural work was rapidly disappearing in an age of mass production. Those who have survived are the craftsmen who have been able to meet the challenge of changing circumstances by becoming qualified agricultural engineers, using modern equipment and modern techniques of manufacture. Most are concerned with the maintenance and repair of factory-made commodities.

Interior of blacksmith's shop, Cenarth, Dyfed (*Welsh Folk Museum*)

Griff Jenkins of Cwrtnewydd, Dyfed, 1975 (*Welsh Folk Museum*)

The Tinsmith

The craft of the tinsmith has virtually disappeared from the countryside and few representatives of this once common trade may be seen at work today. To many, the craft of manipulating tinplate is a semi-skilled occupation carried out by itinerant tinkers, who at one time wandered from district to district to repair hollow kitchen ware. But the craft had its highly skilled aspects and the maker of tinware was an essential member of both a rural and urban community. The tinsmith was responsible for making a variety of tinned goods and the craft reached its most flourishing period during the second half of the nineteenth century, with the availability of tinplate from a flourishing metal industry in such places as South Wales. Although tinsmiths were fairly common in the early nineteenth century, it was really after 1860 that they became really numerous, and tinware rapidly replaced wooden and pottery vessels in many a country home. Crafts, such as white coopering, rapidly disappeared as more and more tinned utensils were used in the dairy and kitchen. Milking pails, cream separators and butter churns which were traditionally made of sycamore or oak were rapidly ousted by tinned utensils, and vessels for carrying water, oil and milk were usually of tin rather than of pottery or wood.

The craft of tinsmithing, although widely distributed throughout the land, was to a great extent an occupation of the market town rather than the countryside; indeed, many of the tinned utensils used in country districts emanated from workshops in industrial towns, in close proximity to the tinplate works. In South Wales, for example, Ebbw Vale and the Rhondda Valley were important centres of tinsmithing and the craftsmen were responsible not only for supplying industrial communities with such necessities as tea jacks and food boxes for coal miners, but also for such things as milk pails and water jacks for the rural population of the Welsh countryside. In South Wales, only one tinsmith, Arnold Cole of Mountain Ash, Mid-Glamorgan, still remains at work, and he still produces a wide range of necessities that are marketed in all parts of the country.

Tinsmiths used tools and numerous items of fixed equipment, quite unlike those used by any other craftsman. They required a wide range of purpose-built hand tools—tin strippers and hammers, tongs and soldering irons—together with presses and guillotines, tin-rolling machines and beading jennies and a variety of peculiarly shaped anvils and heating stoves of unusual design.

Arnold Cole, tinsmith, of Mountain Ash, Mid-Glamorgan, marking out tin (*Welsh Folk Museum*)

Cutting tin on guillotine (*Welsh Folk Museum*)

Snipping tin (*Welsh Folk Museum*)

In some districts, especially the Pontypool district of Gwent, the tinsmiths of the locality became famous for the production of decorative boxes, trays and other objects which are today greatly prized by antique collectors. The making of japanned ware demanded great care and the Pontypool craftsmen became highly skilled. The object to be made was first shaped and then washed in a solution of water and *aqua fortis* to produce a perfectly clean surface. After heating the tin, coat after coat of clear and coloured varnish were applied to the surface, and beautifully executed paintings of flowers and houses were painted on the object, with the result that it was difficult to believe that the object in question started off as an ordinary piece of tin.

Not all the tinsmiths of the countryside could reach the level of perfection attained by the craftsmen of Pontypool. Most were concerned with producing the utilitarian necessities of home, farm and factory.

Saddlers

Just as the blacksmith was essential in the horse age to ensure that farm animals were well shod and the tillage implements they drew performed effectively, the saddler was essential to see that the horses were correctly harnessed to draw those implements. So great was the demand for horse harness that three categories of craftsmen were employed in the saddlery trade. The first was the saddler, responsible for making riding and draught saddles, obtaining the frames of saddles from another specialist, the saddle-tree maker, who was usually an urban craftsman. The second craftsman was the horse-collar maker, while the third, the harness maker, was responsible for producing the numerous straps and bands required in horse harness.

With the rapid disappearance of the horse as a draught animal from British farms, especially in the nineteen-thirties and forties, the work for each individual craftsman became less and less and the far fewer number that remained in the saddlery trade had to spread their activities over a much wider field to produce other goods apart from horse harness. In addition, there was a rapid decline in saddlery as a true country craft and the dwindling number of saddlers were usually to be found in workshops which were located in market towns. Most of those who are at work in country towns today are principally repairers of leather goods, that may range from briefcases to footballs, for much of the harness required for riding horses rather than draught animals is usually produced by manufacturers from Walsall, which has always been the main centre of leather production in Britain. It is only in places such as Newbury and Newmarket, which are in close proximity to racing stables, that the craft of saddlery seems as flourishing as ever. Nevertheless, the popularity of riding and pony trekking has brought a revival to the saddlery trade and the few craftsmen left in the craft have encountered ever-increasing difficulty in meeting the modern demand for riding harness. The category of work that

has really disappeared is that of making heavy harness for draught animals, and although the horse population of Britain is increasing year by year, there has been no corresponding increase in the number of saddlers.

According to some old country saddlers, a set of horse harness is very much like a pair of shoes; it must be fitted to the horse for which it is intended and should never be placed on any other horse. It is very rarely that one will find harness which will properly fit two horses. In the past when heavy harness was used almost daily, year in and year out, it was said that every set should be renovated, overhauled and even rebuilt once every year, for leather always stretched and strained and would in places wear very quickly. This was particularly true of the collar, which took a heavy strain in drawing an implement or vehicle. It was vital that the inner surface of the collar, which was stuffed with straw and flannel, should be perfectly smooth, for an uneven surface would cause irritation and sores on the animal's neck.

One of the main secrets of a saddler's trade is his ability to make the best possible use of a hide with as little wastage as possible. One of the first things an apprentice saddler has to learn is to plan a hide so as to get the most out of it. 'One has to understand leather,' said an old country saddler; 'one has to plan each cut for the particular part of the harness for which its thickness and strength are best suited.'

No craftsman possesses more tools than the saddler and many of those that he uses are peculiar to his trade. In the distant past, these tools were made by country blacksmiths, but for many years the large-scale manufacturers of Walsall have held a monopoly in the supply of leather-making tools. Thus the equipment of the country saddler is virtually standardised throughout Britain and there are few regional variations in tool design.

A great variety of leathers are used in the saddlery trade, most of the best-quality riding saddles being of pigskin, but the most common is brown leather

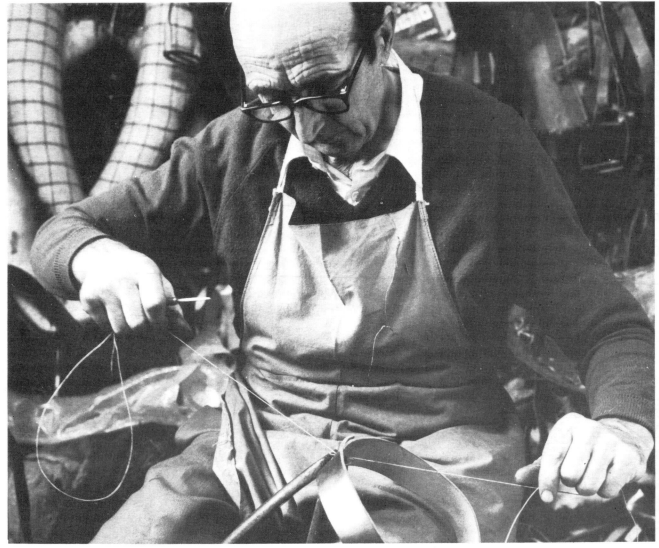

Geler Jones, saddler, Cardigan, Dyfed, sewing a harness strap, 1975 (*Welsh Folk Museum*)

from the backs of cattle. 'Harness backs', as they are called, are of high quality and can be cut into straps of considerable length. For cart-horse harness, however, the leather is dyed black and can be greased time and time again to maintain its supple qualities. The craftsman also uses many types and thicknesses of thread, ranging from simple hemp thread to fine silk thread for saddles, riding bridles and martingales. Since the saddler requires a variety of thread thicknesses for his work, he waxes and twists his own thread; indeed this was one of the first practical tasks that every apprentice had to learn. Although beeswax was used for making the best-quality white thread, the usual wax is made of pitch, resin and linseed oil.

Stuffing a horse collar (*Welsh Folk Museum*)

Shearing at Dolgellau, Gwynedd, *c.* 1910

TEXTILE WORKERS

The craft of weaving cloth is the most widespread and important of rural industries. In the past it was impossible to move any distance at all without meeting some evidence of the existence of this important industry. The weaver, whether he worked in the home or in a factory building, was as essential to the rural community as the blacksmith or carpenter. There was hardly a parish or village which did not have its contingent of spinners, carders, fullers, knitters and weavers.

But in addition to those textile workers who supplied the rural community with its day-to-day essentials, in some parts of the country, especially the West of England, East Anglia, Yorkshire and Mid-Wales, the textile crafts became industries of major importance. All developed from the small mills of the craftsman weavers that were to be found in every region. While the woollen industry in the industrialised conurbations displayed a highly developed division of labour and factory specialisation, in the small rural factories there was no such specialisation and usually all the processes of manufacture were concentrated in one building. The specialised carding and spinning mills of Yorkshire and the dye works and weaving factories of Wessex were rare in the truly rural areas.

The Esgair Moel Woollen Mill preserved at the Welsh Folk Museum, St Fagans, is typical of the small type of rural mill that once dotted the Welsh countryside. The factory is a long, whitewashed stone building typical of the all-purpose rural woollen mill that sprang up in most parts of Wales during the second half of the eighteenth century. The mill was primarily concerned with supplying a local market and it never entered the highly competitive trade channelled to such centres as London, Liverpool and Shrewsbury. Local farmers brought their fleeces to the mill; it was spun into yarn and woven into cloth or blankets for the farmers' families. The manufacturer made no money charge at all for his services, but he kept a proportion of the fleeces that farmers brought in for processing, which he wove into cloth and blankets for sale to the general public at fairs and markets.

Dyers

Before the advent of synthetic dyes, textile workers used a variety of vegetable, flower and other natural dyes. The art of dyeing goes back to prehistoric times and natural dyes such as woad, indigo and whortleberries were well known to ancient civilisations.

The stage in production at which wool is dyed varies according to the preferences of the textile worker and the type of cloth to be woven. In some cases raw wool, sometimes scoured, sometimes in the grease, is dyed before carding. In the past, this was done in large, open vats and the worker would stir the boiling dye and wool at frequent intervals with a pole. In the smaller rural factories, this method of dyeing still persists. At the Esgair Moel Mill from Llanwrtyd, Brecknockshire, for example, the usual method is to dye unwashed raw wool in a large thirty-gallon copper vat. The dye vat is always heated with wood fires and there is a tradition in Brecknock that the best timber for heating purposes is alder, which up to 1939 could be obtained from the itinerant clog-sole makers who frequently visited the alder groves of the county and sold waste timber locally. The practice of dyeing raw wool in the grease has a distinct disadvantage in that the rollers of the carding engines have to be cleaned at frequent intervals, to ensure that one colour does not contaminate another. This is particularly true where white wool follows a strongly coloured one through the carding set.

As an alternative to dyeing the raw wool, the fibres may be dyed at the yarn stage, either in the form of hanks suspended from rods or in the form of packages known as 'cheeses' or 'cones'. These packages consist of a pound of yarn wound on bobbins and immersed in a dyeing vat. Since there is no movement of the yarn in the dyeing, the wool does not become felted, as in the other processes. Cheese dyeing is preferred in cases where fine yarn is required.

A great many woollen cloths are dyed in piece form—that is, as lengths of woven cloth. In many mills a wooden winch with a cranked handle is fixed above the dye vat and this was used for rolling the dyed cloth from the vat below. In the eighteenth century, the flannel of Mid-Wales for example, if it was to be coloured at all, was usually piece-dyed by the dyers employed by the Drapers' Company of Shrewsbury.

Wool is a highly reactive substance and no difficulty is experienced in bringing about combination with dyes. Before synthetic dyes were available—the first one was discovered in 1856—textile manufacturers throughout the world were dependent on natural dyes. They depended on a great variety of vegetable dyes such as madder, foxgloves and lichens, together with different metallic mordants such as iron, alum and tin. With these natural dyes, the range of colours was extremely limited and considerable variation and unevenness could exist where the vegetable matter was harvested at different times of the year. Colour could also vary considerably according to the length of time the wool was boiled in the dyeing liquid. On the whole, the colours produced by vegetable dyes on their own were rather dull and lifeless. Very often too the methods of mixing dyes depended as much on guesswork as on recipes passed down over many generations.

A wide variety of colours could be obtained from simple raw materials. The quantity of dye included in the vat, the length of boiling and the time of year when the plants were picked could all affect the final colour of wool. Birch leaves, for example, were best used in the early spring. If fresh leaves were used, then the weight of leaves should have been equal to the weight of wool. On the other hand, if the dyer used dried leaves, then he would need four times the weight of wool to be dyed. The leaves had to be soaked for twenty-four hours and the wool boiled in the solution for no more than an hour. This would produce a yellow wool, but if boiling were to go on for a longer period, the wool would turn green. If the birch-dyed wool was mordanted with alum, the resultant colour would be a bright yellow; chrome mordanting would produce tan, and iron or copperas mordanting a blackish brown. In general, the longer wool was boiled, the darker it became. The following are some examples of the colours produced by dyers to the end of the nineteenth century.

Dark Brown Yellow wall lichen; red currants (with alum); crottle; bracken (with chrome or alum); privet (with copperas); sorrel (on its own or with chrome, alum or copperas); walnut shells; dock (with alum or copperas); blackberry (with gall nuts).

Tans and Light Browns Lichens (on their own or with alum, chrome or tin); sloe berries; elderberry;

birch leaves (with chrome); broom flowers (with copperas); bracken; weld (with copperas); privet (with chrome); bedstraw (with chrome); onion skin; heather (with chrome).

Blues Blueberry (with copperas); elder (with alum); indigo; woad.

Black The most popular method was to boil copperas with gall nuts, oak bark or sawdust.

Greens Gorse; privet berries (with salt); iris leaf; broom; heather (with indigo); unripe blackthorn; birch leaves. It was very difficult to obtain a good green colour, and more often than not wool was dyed blue and then yellow or vice versa

Purples Blueberry (with alum); bitter vetch; blackberry.

Yellows: Leaves of apple, ash, buckthorn, hazel, birch (with alum); bracken root; St John's wort; rock lichen; dog's mercury; gorse; weld (on its own or if darker colours were required, with tin, chrome or alum); privet (with alum); heather (with alum); bedstraw (with alum); nettles (with alum).

Orange Ragweed; bramble.

Magenta Dandelion.

Reds Bedstraw roots; madder; tormentil roots; foxgloves; cochineal; lichens (with ammonia).

There were, of course, countless variations in colour, some of them demanding the admixture of numerous elements and many hours of preparation.

Carders and Spinners

Carding is the process of opening out the fibres of wool so that the fleece is completely disentangled and every fibre is free and even. Before the introduction of water-driven carding machinery in the late eighteenth century, carding was a hand process carried out with a pair of cards. The word carding is derived from the Latin *carduus*—thistle; thistle heads inserted in a frame being used for the process in the past. By far the most common type of hand card, however, was one made up of teasels. Four or six teasel heads were fixed in rectangular, handled wooden frames and used in pairs to loosen and disentangle wool. Since the thirteenth century metal-covered cards were well known in Britain, and until the beginning of the nineteenth century, and even later in some districts, they were by far the most common implements for domestic carding. Each hand card consisted of a leather-covered wooden board covered with rows of inclined teeth or staples. Wool was placed on one card and pulled apart gently with the teeth of the other. This was done a number of times until a short, spongy sliver of wool was produced.

The late eighteenth century saw a revolution in the woollen industry, for it saw the introduction of the water-driven carding engine which soon ousted the hand cards of metal or teasels which had been used for the process since the dawn of history. Carding had to become a factory process and, as a result, in all parts of Britain fewer and fewer people became concerned with domestic carding in cottages and farmhouses, for the new machines required water power for driving them.

The carding engine with its series of revolving rollers was first patented by Daniel Bourn, a Leominster cotton manufacturer, and his invention was improved upon by Lewis Paul, a London shroud maker. The famous Richard Arkwright was responsible for improving the carding engine still further around 1775 and it is machines based on his designs that are still widely used in the woollen industry.

The process of carding actually consists of two operations: that of the initial disentangling or scribbling and the condensing of the wool fibres in the carding engine proper. One disadvantage of the early carders was the fact that the wool was delivered in short, thick rolls of the same width as the scribbler

Carding engine at the Esgair Moel Mill (*Welsh Folk Museum*)

Mule spinning at the Esgair Moel Mill (*Welsh Folk Museum*)

itself. The slivers had to be pieced together in longer rolls by hand, a task usually performed by children, known as 'pieceners'. This was arduous work and 'very often,' said a writer in 1805, 'was seen the backs of the children's hands red with blood from wounds inflicted from rolling the rolls of wool continuously day after day.' The introduction of the piecing machine in the 1820s dispensed with the need for pieceners and improvements in carding condensers ensured that uniform lengths of slubbing were produced ready for spinning.

Before carded wool can be used for weaving, it has to be made strong and elastic enough to bear considerable strain and friction. The preparation of carded wool for weaving is the process of spinning, where each individual fibre is twisted firmly around the next while at the same time the sliver is extended. Although in prehistoric times spinning may have been performed by rolling wool fibre between the hands, spinning with spindle and distaff has been known in Britain for many centuries. The equipment was very simple, consisting of nothing more than a wooden distaff for holding the fibre of wool and a weighted spindle for winding the spun yarn. A woman, and spinning is traditionally a woman's task, could spin yarn as she walked or watched a flock of sheep or a herd of cattle. It was a slow, laborious process and spinning was mechanised fairly early on by the widespread adoption of the spinning wheel, which was among the first devices involving continuous rotary action. Variations of the spinning wheel, some in the form of treadle wheels, others in the form of 'great' wheels without treadles, were the only devices used for spinning until the late eighteenth century. The earliest machine to be adopted was James Hargreaves's famous jenny, which spun twenty or more threads simultaneously, but this was soon followed by Samuel Crompton's mule and its various improvements. Mule spinning, usually on automatic machines, is still by far the most common method of spinning today.

Weavers

A piece of cloth is made up of longitudinal threads laid parallel to one another, constituting the 'warp' or 'chain'. These, which are placed in the loom first, are stretched between two beams and are intersected by transverse threads known as the 'weft', 'woof', 'filling' or 'pick'. The process of weaving consists of inserting the threads of the weft between the alternate threads of the warp. However intricate a loom may be, whether it is operated by hand or electric power, the essential parts and operations are the same.

All looms require warp threads, which are generally stronger than the weft threads. These are specially prepared in an operation known as 'warping'. For centuries, until the evolution of the warping mill in the mid-nineteenth century, the process was performed on pegs stuck in the ground or on a vertical framework attached to the wall of a building. In some districts it was customary to prepare warp threads by treating them with size often prepared by boiling rabbit skins in water. Inserting the warp in the loom, a process known as 'beaming', is an intricate and painfully slow task, requiring considerable skill. Great care has to be taken to ensure that every thread is inserted with equal tension or the texture of the finished cloth will be uneven.

Excluding the primitive warp-weighted loom, which seems to have disappeared from England and Wales by the later Middle Ages, the simplest form of loom is the hand loom, of a type which persisted in the remoter, smaller mills until quite recently. The Esgair Moel Woollen Mill, for example, has two looms, the one capable of turning out cloth eighty-eight inches wide, the other fifty-four inches wide. The four upright parts of each loom are joined together by two long and two short horizontal posts. At the back, or the end farthest away from the weaver, is a roller known as a 'warp beam' and the threads of the warp are carefully rolled on this to extend forwards, possibly over another horizontal roller, through the grooved beam, to the 'cloth beam' at the front of the

D.J. Davies weaving on a handloom at the Esgair Moel Mill, Welsh Folk Museum, St Fagans, 1969 (*Welsh Folk Museum*)

Tom Rees of Maesllyn Mills, Dyfed, weaving a bedcover, 1963 (*Welsh Folk Museum*)

loom. In the middle the warp passes through a series of vertical threads or, in recent times, wires stretched between upright bars. These are the 'healds' or 'heddles', which on the larger loom number 323. Each set of healds is known as a 'leaf' and each leaf is connected to one of the foot treadles by wooden pulleys, slats and cords. Both looms at Esgair Moel are equipped with four treadles and a pattern of considerable complexity may be woven on them. To raise the heddles and, consequently, the warp threads, one of the pedals is pressed, the leaf lifts and the weft thread is inserted. In addition, the warp threads are inserted in the 'comb' or 'reed' carried by the movable 'batten' or 'sley'. Several of the threads are passed through each division of the reed to keep them in position. The weaver sits on the bench attached to the back of the loom and, after pressing the appropriate treadle to lift a section of the warp, the shuttle is placed in the shuttle box on the sley and thrown across to complete the weft. The shuttle itself is a piece of hardwood tapering to a point at each end, with a cavity in the centre for the bobbin. This is a small wooden pipe on which is wound a quantity of weft. As the shuttle shoots across the warp, the weft is unravelled from the bobbin and it unwinds through a small hole in the slot of the shuttle. To throw the shuttle a piece of string or cloth hanging in front of the weaver is pulled. This is attached to thick pieces of very hard leather, which slide upon short spindles in the shuttle boxes at either end of the batten. When the string is pulled the piece of leather, which is called a 'picker', strikes the shuttle, and causes it to shoot across with considerable force to the other end. The weft thread is beaten home and packed close by the batten and the reeds that it carries, and the process is continued until a long length of cloth has been rolled on the cloth beam.

In many cases, and particularly if the weaver is concerned with weaving further lengths of the same material, the old warp will not be removed. The craftsman cuts across the warp near the warp beam and

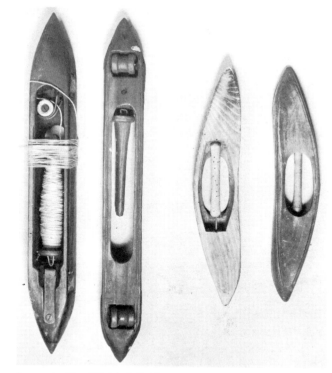

Loom shuttles (*Welsh Folk Museum*)

Museum of the Welsh Woollen Industry at Cambrian Mill, Drefach, Llandysul, Dyfed (*Welsh Folk Museum*)

83

threads of the new warp are tied to the thrums of the old.

The first power loom was produced by Edmund Cartwright in 1785. In this, all the parts were motivated by power, first by that of an ox, then by water and then by steam engine. During the early part of the nineteenth century, many looms of different designs were patented, but even so hand-loom weaving persisted in many parts of Britain until well into the nineteenth century. Take the case of the small Mid-Wales market town of Newtown, the 'Leeds of Wales' to early nineteenth-century travellers. The tall, three- or four-floored buildings with their many windows bear witness to this day to the importance of the weaving industry in the history of Montgomeryshire. A weaving factory, occupying the third and fourth floors of a building, stretched over many cottage dwellings and could be entered by an outside staircase at the back of the terrace. In many cases the owner of a weaving factory was also the owner of a shop at the end of the row, and on applying for work, a weaver was always asked for the number of persons in his family; the bigger the family, the better were his chances of obtaining work. The average wage in 1837 was eleven shillings a week, and according to a contemporary observer the prices paid in the truck shops were considerably higher than those paid in the market or other shops for 'the masters take care not to pay their men until the market has been closed, thus virtually compelling them to take the whole of the article consumed at their price. I have often seen men sneaking to other places to buy the same as they were going to steal.'

In weaving, considerable varieties of texture and interlacings of thread may occur, but the principal types of weave are:

Plain Weave This is the simplest form of weave, made by interlacing the warp with the weft, alternately over and under as in simple basketry. The firm cloth produced is exactly the same in appearance on both sides, and most of the flannels and 'homespuns' produced by many rural mills fall into this category. The texture can be varied by using heavier threads for the warp.

Twill Weave If the warp and weft threads are interlaced so that the weft passes under two and over two warp threads, a diagonal line is produced across the surface of the cloth. Twill weaves can vary tremendously. The herring-bone design in tweeds, for example, is obtained by this method.

Double Cloth Weave The well-known multi-coloured *carthenni* produced by many Welsh mills at the present time and incorrectly called 'tapestry quilts' are of this type. Two cloths are woven on the loom at the same time, each with its own set of warp and of filling, and joined invisibly by extra warp or filling threads interlacing them together. Frequently, the two sets of yarns weave separately to form the figure, then combine to make the background.

FOOD AND DRINK MAKERS

In the past, in most districts, the countryman was able to grow all the food that he, his family and neighbours required. His fields, gardens and orchards supplied him with ample quantities of corn, vegetables and fruit; his animals gave him milk and meat. Until recent times such tasks as baking bread, making butter, cheese, cider and beer were very much a part of the household routine of most farms. Pigs were killed and salted in all districts while many products of the farms—corn, wool or animal skins—could be taken to a nearby mill for processing. The products of those mills could either be used in the home or by another craftsman to produce some essentials.

Corn Millers

One of the most widespread of all rural crafts was that of corn milling, and a water- or wind-driven mill was to be found in almost every parish in the land.

Perhaps the most exciting-looking of all types of mill is the windmill, found in low-lying, flat districts such as East Anglia, where turgid streams can hardly provide enough power to drive any machinery at all. The earliest windmills, dating back to the twelfth century, were undoubtedly solid towers built to face the prevailing winds. If the wind changed direction, then the mills could not be operated. The post mill, an example of which has been preserved at the Avoncroft Museum of Buildings, was a distinct improvement on the static tower, for the all-wooden mill was pivoted on a heavy upright post and the whole building could be manhandled to face the wind. Brick or stone tower mills with rotating wooden caps were a later development, while the smock mill with a brick base and wooden superstructure was an eighteenth-century improvement. In early windmills the lattice work of revolving sails (and milling terms were always maritime terms) were equipped with removable cloth that could be adjusted according to the strength of the wind. Another eighteenth-century device was the fantail, a set of rotary vanes set at right angles to the sails to turn those sails in the correct direction to face the wind.

In some districts, notably the East Anglian coast and Milford Haven, corn mills depended on the flow of the tide to drive machinery. The Woodbridge Tide Mill in Suffolk has been renovated and is typical of the once commonplace mills found in tidal estuaries in the past. Tides provide a reliable, endless and regular, though intermittent, source of energy. Water mills, on the banks of flowing rivers, suffer from severe frost, floods and drought, whereas tide mills are only endangered by sea storms. It was only natural, therefore, that the inhabitants of coastal areas should have tried to harness tides as a source of energy.

By far the most common type of mill was the water mill. An example from Dyfed has been preserved at

Melin Bompren, a Dyfed corn mill now at the Welsh Folk Museum (*Welsh Folk Museum*)

the Welsh Folk Museum. The mill is typical of the small stone-built mills that once dotted the Welsh countryside. Like most other Welsh mills, Melin Bompren is a stone-built, hip-roofed building on three floors with a lower building containing a kiln for corn drying attached. The mill is built on a slope, so that at the back only two floors appear above the ground while at the front it has three floors. A narrow doorway at the back leads to the first floor, or 'stone floor', of the mill, while at the front another door, located on the pine end of the building, is wide enough to admit a cart to the ground floor. The all-iron, overshot water wheel was made by S. F. Kelly of Cardigan, and a wooden trough, whose angle may be controlled by a lever on the first floor, leads from the mill race and pond. The flow of water along the mill race is controlled by a wooden trap door. Not only does the wheel drive the machinery but it also provides power for the chain hoist, by which sacks of grain were lifted from the ground floor through two pairs of hinged trap doors in the other floors to the top of the building or 'bin floor'.

The top floor itself was for storing grain and it contains the entrances of four chutes leading to the milling machinery on the first or 'stone' floor. The first of these pieces of milling machinery is a pair of French burr millstones, usually preferred for milling barley, a cereal crop which was especially important in south Cardiganshire before 1914. Millstone grit stones were preferred for wheat and oat milling and Melin Bompren has a pair of well-used stones of this type. The quality of a millstone is of vital importance to the miller and both the fixed bed stones and the revolving runner stone had to be dressed at regular intervals with a special hammer known as a 'mill bill'. Deep grooves of a regular pattern had to be cut in the stone to ensure that they ground the corn efficiently and distributed the flour at the periphery of the stone. A home-made gauge consisting of a piece of wood with a feather marker for testing the true running of the stones was

an essential piece of equipment in stone dressing. Both pairs of stones are enclosed on a wooden casing with hoppers for feeding the grain above. On the first floor of the building, too, is the grain cleaner, for when seed was brought into the mill for grinding it was hauled from the ground floor of the building to the top floor by means of the chain hoist. Before it could be milled, impurities had to be removed and the grain had to be passed through the cleaner, with its series of oscillating sieves, to remove all the materials which could not be milled. The cleaned grain came out of the seed cleaner through a chute to the ground floor of the building, where it was sacked and hoisted again to the top floor. The other piece of equipment on the first floor is a flour bolter which, with its series of revolving brushes, was used for refining flour and ensuring that the best and finest grained flour was separated from the bran and inferior flour. On the first floor, too, the mill's main driving gear with apple-wood cogs on cast-iron wheels is located, together with the revolving shaft, connected to the water wheel.

On the ground floor are found the chutes and troughs for the milled flour and husks, together with a winnower, mainly used for winnowing oats. In this, oats were sieved to separate the husks from the flour. The room adjoining the mill is the kiln where oats were gently heated for some hours before milling. A fire was lit in the grate underneath a metal-bottomed, perforated grain container, the walls of the device being of stone. The oats were placed on the metal, a fire of anthracite dust lit underneath and the oats gently heated, the grain being gently mixed every twenty minutes or so with a long-handled wooden rake. Usually oats were roasted for three hours and, after cooling for twelve hours or more, the grain was milled. It was then winnowed and the oat kernels were again milled. Occasionally the husks too were milled. Oatmeal was, of course a staple diet in West Wales.

Maltsters

In many parts of the country the remains of malt-houses may still be seen. These range from small buildings attached to farms where malt for domestic beer brewing was prepared, to huge maltings where malt for large-scale breweries was produced.

The main ingredient of all types of beer is traditionally malt, derived from barley. Malting is in reality a speeded-up process of what takes place when barley is planted in the soil. In the maltings, the maltster makes use of this natural process of growth, but in such a way that the growth is under very strict control. Farmhouse malting was a task usually undertaken in the winter when barley, after being steeped in water for approximately five days, was drained and spread evenly over the dry floor of perforated tiles in the malt-house. It was left there without being touched for a period varying between twelve and forty-eight hours, depending on the temperature, until the first appearance of small roots emanating from the base of the corn. From that stage, great care had to be taken, the temperature had to be controlled and the sprouting grain had to be turned at frequent intervals with wooden shovels and rakes. No one, unless he was barefooted, was allowed on the growing floor, in case the barley was damaged, for damaged corn was quite likely to become mouldy and useless. The process of flooring went on for about ten days and occasionally water was sprinkled on it.

The 'green' malt was taken to a kiln, placed on the perforated tiles and gently dried by the wood fire lit in the chamber beneath. The heating arrested growth and gave the malt its characteristic 'biscuity' taste.

Brewers

The basis of good beer is malted barley, and brewing is still practised as a domestic pursuit in many parts of the country. In parts of Dyfed, for example, domestic brewing is still widely practised, and to make the strong beer of Christmas, eight or nine gallons of clean spring water are heated to near boiling point.

For the brew of harvest-time, however, weaker beer is required and the amount of water is increased to fifteen gallons for every bushel of malt. The water is then poured on the malt in a wooden or copper vat. A bunch of gorse or of wheat straw is fitted over the bung hole at the bottom of the vessel to act as a filter when the liquid is drained. The mixture is allowed to cool for about three hours. In the meantime another consignment of water, about ten gallons, is boiled, added to the vat and allowed to cool. A quantity of liquid is drawn from the vat, and hops and sugar are added after boiling. After cooling overnight, yeast is added and the beer is left to ferment for a few days before casking or bottling.

The process of brewing even in the largest brewery is basically the same as in farmhouse brewhouses. Malt is crushed to crack the grain and break up the starch content. The crushed malt or 'grist' is mixed with hot water in a so-called 'mash tun' and left for some hours under strict control to mix. The malt extract or 'wort' is strained and run off into large coppers to be boiled for about two hours. Hops are added and, after cooling, the chopped wort is pumped into a large fermenting vessel where yeast is added. The fermentation of draught beer takes about a week and during that period the yeast breaks down the malt sugars and the added sugars and converts them into alcohol and carbon dioxide. The wort itself is converted into beer.

Cider Makers

Like beer brewing, the farmhouse cider making is still widely practised in some parts of the country, although there has been a sharp decline in the craft and in the number of cider orchards in the countryside. Not long ago extensive orchards containing such varieties of apple as Golden Pippin, Redstreak, Old Foxwhelp and others were well distributed throughout the country, especially in the West of England, Sussex, Hereford and Monmouth, but many of those orchards have been destroyed in recent years.

Travelling cider makers in Herefordshire (*E. Warrilow*)

To make farmhouse cider, apples are harvested in October and November; the fruit is not usually picked from the trees by hand, but the trees themselves are shaken, so that the ripe apples fall to the ground. They are then heaped in the orchard to mature and rot for a week or two before pressing.

The traditional method of milling apples is to use a stone mill, consisting of a massive circular trough, in which runs a large, horse-driven stone crushing wheel. The horse or donkey is harnessed head first into the shafts which are connected to the crushing vessel. As soon as the trough is filled with apples, the horse begins walking around it, pushing the wheel to crush the apples.

The pomace, after being crushed thoroughly, is transferred with wooden shovels to the press, usually a massive oak-framed apparatus at the base of which is a heavy stone slab. This is grooved near the outer edge and has a lip projecting over a stone or wooden vat. A straw, goat-hair or horsehair mat is placed on the slab and the pomace shovelled on it. Another mat is placed above this and more pomace on that. In this way, layers of pomace are arranged in the press and the central screw is wound down to exert full pressure on the layers of pomace. Juices filter through the mats, dripping into the groove of the stone and into the vat below.

The cider is then casked and allowed to ferment. In the past it was a common practice to boil spent pomace in water to produce an inferior fermented drink called 'ciderkin'.

FISHERMEN

Fishing for a wide range of freshwater and sea fish has provided a livelihood for many generations of riverside and coastal dwellers, and many rural crafts came into being in order to supply the needs of the fisherman. Ropemaking, for example, was widely practised and persisted longer in fishing ports than anywhere else, while specialised skills like constructing coracles and fishing traps have persisted until the present day in certain districts. A great deal of the equipment required by fishermen is traditionally made by the fishermen themselves, and most netsmen, for example, are capable of producing the nets that they require, although the majority today purchase nets from large-scale manufacturers. In all cases, however, to comply with local regulations regarding size and mesh of nets large-scale manufacturers at such places as Bridport in Dorset have to make nets to the specifications of fishermen from a particular river.

Angling Equipment Makers

Angling is the most popular of all sports, and a great variety of tackle may be purchased or made and a great variety of techniques may be adopted for the capture of fish. Although much of the fishing tackle used by hundreds of anglers today is factory produced, home-made equipment was commonplace until recently. For example, many anglers are proficient in the art of fly tying, and with scissors and pliers, silk thread and coloured feathers and hair, there are many experts who can produce perfect examples of fishing flies. Until the nineteen-thirties, in some parts of the country, the actual fishing hooks themselves were made by fishermen. These were simply cut out of a piece of blackthorn and baked in an oven so as to harden the points. In some districts, anglers used lugworm as bait and a worm was threaded from the bottom of a hook upwards and over the point of a thorn.

Modern barbed hooks are produced by large-scale manufacturers principally in the Redditch district, the home of the needle industry; indeed, Redditch developed as the main centre of manufacturing other angling equipment—rods, lines and gut, for example. The hooks are attached to the main fishing line by a length of gut or nylon known as 'a snood' and, in the past, snoods as well as the lines themselves were made of horsehair, or a mixture of silk thread, horsehair and plaited silk. Best horsehair, it was said, was obtained from a young chestnut horse with a flaxen tail. To make a fishing line, a bunch of horsehair was divided into three, and each bunch, possibly six hairs in each, was passed through three sections of a goose quill and plaited.

Fishing rods have been known for centuries and a book published in 1496 describes how a rod was made in two parts—a 'staffe' and a 'croppe'. Hazel, willow or rowan was used for the staff or butt and this was cut in winter, when there was no sap in the tree. The rod was hardened and straightened by tying it to another rod and allowing it to dry in the smoke of an open chimney. A tapering piece of wood, as thick as a man's arm at the bottom, was preferred and the pith was burnt out with a hot metal poker to make a hollow rod. The top or crop was kept inside the butt when not in use. The top was, and often still is, made in two parts, which together are equal to the length of the butt. The lower part of the top was usually of green hazel, the upper part of blackthorn, crabtree, medlar or juniper. Until the seventeenth century, reels were unknown and horsehair lines were lashed to the tips of the rods. Hazel, split cane, greenheart and more recently fibre-glass and aluminium have been used to make rods, but only a few are the product of rural workshops today.

Fishing flies date back to prehistoric times and as early as the second century BC hooks with pieces of coloured cloth and feathers tied to them were used in Greece. For trout fishing today, the aim of the fisherman is to catch the fish by presenting them with more or less the exact imitation of the food on which they happen to be feeding at any one time. Dry-fly fishing is concerned with the imitation of the actual flies which float on the surface of the water, while wet-fly fishing may represent the larval stage of those flies, beetles, caterpillars or drowned flies. Unlike the trout, the salmon does not feed in fresh water so it would be pointless to imitate the flies of the riverside in making artificial bait. Colourful lures of exotic feathers, tinsel and silk or lures that resemble wispy wings of hair and feathers show the fly tier's art at its best.

Basket Trappers

One of the oldest methods of catching fish is in fixed weirs, built especially along the seashore or in rivers for the capture of a variety of fish. But in addition to semi-permanent weirs of stone and wattle, there are also in many parts of the country removable traps which are set up during a fishing season only. The most notable of these are the basket traps of the Severn estuary, which were legalised by an Act of 1865. The most common and widespread of these baskets is the so-called 'putcher', which is a cone-shaped, openly woven willow basket, five feet long and about two feet in diameter at the mouth and tapering to about five inches in diameter at the tip. The putchers, which are used exclusively for salmon catching, are arranged in ranks of several hundred, ranged in three or four tiers to form a weir. Autumn-cut willow is used to make putchers and most are made by the fishermen themselves during the closed fishing season.

The services of a competent basket maker are required to make the second type of basket trap, known as a 'putt'. Each putt of closely woven basketry consists of three sections, known as 'kipe', 'butt' and 'fore-wheel'. They are like three large buckets dove-tailed into one another, and the last one is so closely woven that nothing, even the smallest shrimp, can escape. The diameter of the kipe may be as great as five feet at the mouth and the whole structure may be fifteen feet long. The putts are made of willow, hazel or blackthorn and in use in the Severn estuary they are built in single rows in the tidal section of the river. In both types of basket the incoming tide will cover the whole of the putcher or putt weir and the catch can only be removed at low tide.

Portable eel traps, of wickerwork, are still widely used in the Fens and East Anglia, and these, with a complex arrangement of non-return valves inside them, are usually the products of professional basket makers.

Coracle Men

The use of the coracle as a fishing craft has declined very rapidly in recent years, so that today coracle fishing is limited to three rivers only—the Teifi, Tywi and Tâf, in Dyfed. In the nineteen-thirties coracles were

A putt rank at Shepperdine in the Severn estuary (*Welsh Folk Museum*)

to be found on many other rivers, such as the Dee, Severn and Cleddau, while, during the first decade of this century, most of the sizeable rivers of Wales had coracle fishermen. The Salmon and Freshwater Fisheries Act put an end to coracle fishing on many rivers and severely restricted fishing on many others. Subsequent river authority bye-laws have caused an even more rapid decline in coracle fishing and in some districts the coracle is on the point of disappearing. For example, at Cenarth, on the River Teifi, long regarded as a centre of coracle fishing, legislation in 1935 prohibited the issue of licences to fishermen in the non-tidal reaches of the river, with the result that salmon fishing at Cenarth ceased in 1972. In the tidal reaches of the river, five nets are licensed to fish for salmon at Cilgerran, where the traditional two-man coracle nets and the illegal set nets are used in a picturesque gorge below Cilgerran Castle. On the River Tywi at Carmarthen, twelve pairs of coracles are licensed to fish at nights on the river, while on the Tâf, between St Clears and Laugharne, two nets may be legally used.

The design of coracles and the methods of using them varied considerably from river to river. They varied according to the physical nature of each individual stream, whether it was swiftly flowing or slow moving, whether it had rapids and much rough water and whether it was shallow or deep. Design varied too, according to the preferences of the individual fisherman and whether the fisherman preferred a heavy or light coracle. A Teifi coracle, for example, can weigh as little as twenty-five pounds and as much as thirty-six pounds, while the length can vary from fifty inches to sixty inches. The actual size and weight depend almost entirely on the preferences of the fisherman. Again, on the Dee, two-seater coracles were commonplace in the Llangollen district until the nineteen-fifties, and these coracles, weighing as much as forty pounds, were widely used by anglers for reaching inaccessible sections of river.

It seems that coracles varied according to the in-grained traditions of the various rivers of Wales, for remarkable homogeneity in the design of coracles occurred on the various rivers, and distinct regional types were in existence for many centuries. For example, although the coracles of the Tywi and the nearby Tâf are somewhat similar in shape, the Tâf coracle, designed for use in a fairly narrow, swiftly flowing stream, is heavier than the Tywi variety. Instead of the wattled gunwale of the latter it has a planked gunwale. The Tâf coracle is sharper at the fore-end and flatter at the stern and weighs about thirty-three pounds, compared with a maximum weight of twenty-eight pounds in a Tywi coracle.

Methods of construction, too, varied considerably from river to river. Some coracles, like those of the Teifi and Tywi, have plaited hazel gunwales, others have single or double lath gunwales. To build a Tâf coracle, fo example, a naturally curving branch of a tree, usually an apple tree, was cut and split in half to form the fore-part of the gunwale. Another branch was treated in the same way to form the rear gunwale. Unlike the other coracles of West Wales, it was the gunwale of the Tâf coracle which was formed first. This was bored with a series of holes to receive the fourteen laths of the coracle frame. In Teifi coracles, seven longitudinal and seven cross-laths of cleft willow were steamed, weighted and bent into shape to be inserted in a plaited hazel gunwale, while in Tywi coracles sawn ash laths were generally used. In most types of coracle the number of longitudinal laths varied from six (as on Conwy coracle) to ten (as on Severn coracle) to as many as sixteen (as on Upper Dee coracle). The laths could be of ash or willow and carrying straps could be of leather, as in most types, or of twisted oak saplings, as on the Teifi coracle.

Netsmen and Net Makers

By far the most common method of capturing both sea and river fish is to net them, and in the past most of the nets were braided by the fishermen themselves for their own use. Of course, there is a terrific varia-

J.C. Thomas of Cenarth, Dyfed, preparing laths of a Teifi coracle, 1953 (*Welsh Folk Museum*)

Raymond Rees of Carmarthen framing a Tywi coracle (*Welsh Folk Museum*)

A finished Tywi coracle (*Welsh Folk Museum*)

A net maker at work, Cenarth, Dyfed, *c.* 1938 (*M.L. Wight*)

tion in size and design of nets from one part of the country to the other. Some, like the shore seines used in a large number of river estuaries and drift nets used for catching a variety of fish, are plain rectangular walls of netting that can easily be made by machine. Others, such as coracle nets and the trammel drift nets of the Dee estuary, are far more complex and, due to their special shape, have to be braided by hand. The process of hand braiding demands very little in the way of equipment, but requires considerable dexterity in the manipulation of twine.

Today, most of the nets used in England and Wales are manufactured by a large-scale Bridport manufacturer who is able to produce the variety of netting that local custom amongst fishermen has dictated should be used in the various rivers. Although some fishermen may still braid their own nets from bast fibres, such as hemp and flax, the fishing industry has become heavily dependent on commercially manufactured nets, made from synthetic fibres, such as nylon, terylene and polyethylene.

All the nets purchased from Bridport are machine-made nets produced on a complex multi-shuttled netting loom, with its arrangement of hooks, needles and sinkers which form the meshes of a net. From the twelfth century, Bridport has been the all-important centre of rope and net making in Britain. Undoubtedly one of the main reasons why Bridport became preeminent in the manufacture or cordage was that the soil and climate of Dorset were particularly suitable for the growth of flax and hemp and that the early industry was stimulated by the demands of fishermen and boat builders, who flourished on the Dorset coast. By the end of the sixteenth century, Bridport with its superlative hemp and flax and with its long start over other centres of production, had achieved a virtual monopoly of rope and net production in Britain. Although there was a decline in the industry in the early eighteenth century, the second half of the century saw a return of prosperity, with nets of all kinds, rather than rope, becoming the most important pro-

duct. At the turn of the nineteenth century a contemporary writer noted that 'the manufacture of Bridport perhaps flourishes more than at any other former time and furnishes employment not only for the inhabitants of the town, but for those likewise of the neighbouring villages to the extent of ten miles in circumference. It consists of seines and nets of all sorts, lines, twines and similar cordage and sail cloth.' As in the wool textile trade in Yorkshire, Wales and elsewhere, hemp merchants who organised the manufacturing processes were common in the Bridport district. Samuel Gundry, for example, was a merchant and possibly a banker, who as early as 1665 purchased the hemp crop, issued it to families for conversion into yarn and nets in their homes, and then marketed the goods. Until well on into the nineteenth century, most of the net making was carried on as outwork in the cottages of Bridport and the surrounding countryside, and methods of braiding by hand were handed down the generations from mother to daughter. Net making was organised from a central factory; twine was delivered weekly and the finished nets were collected when next week's work was delivered. John Claridge estimated that in 1793 there were 1800 people concerned in the rope and netting trade in Bridport and a further 7000 in the surrounding countryside.

During the nineteenth century imported hemp replaced the locally grown crop for the manufacture of nets, and the century, too, witnessed the growth of a factory system in the Bridport industry, with new machinery being introduced to spin and hackle fibres and with hand looms—the early ones known as 'jumper looms'—becoming commonplace after 1860. The jumper loom, invented in the eighteen-thirties, was so called because of a wooden pedal on which the operator had to jump. This formed the knot around three rows of hooks and drew twine for the next meshes by means of a long neck-like, barb-tipped shuttle. Thirty families were able to purchase one, and with the purchase of a second loom and hiring an operator, many an individual's cottage workshop de-

Elwyn Brown, of Laugharne, Dyfed, and his son, with a wade net (*Welsh Folk Museum*)

James Sallis of St Dogmaels, Dyfed, a seine netsman, 1970 (*Welsh Folk Museum*)

veloped into a small factory. By 1900 power looms were being introduced into the industry and factory production of nets was in the hands of fifteen family firms. Today the work of supplying most of the netting requirements of the fishing industry is in the hands of one large-scale manufacturer, although a certain amount of domestic manufacture is still practised. Despite looms which tie knots at unbelievable rates, the net-making industry still has to fall back on outworking skills which are based on pure pre-Industrial Revolution cottage industry, and has to dispatch vans daily to take out the raw material, collect the finished nets and pay for them.

Traditionally, hemp twine was preferred by all fishermen for fishing nets, but between the two world wars low-priced cotton was widely used. It was regarded as being much lighter than hemp, despite its inferior strength. Since 1945 synthetic fibres have become increasingly more important in the netting industry, although for some nets, such as coracle nets and Dee trammel nets, fishermen still insist on traditional materials. Nets of nylon, terylene and polyethylene have, according to some, many disadvantages. They are affected by sunlight; some create static electricity; and many, being made of very thin twine, can cut off the heads of fish. It is not surprising, therefore, that some fishermen still braid their own nets from hemp and cotton and equip them with headlines of horsehair and cow-hair, much in the manner of past centuries.

LEATHER WORKERS

Tanners

One of the oldest of rural crafts is that of leather tanning and as far back as the Stone Age primitive man knew how to scrape, dry and oil animal skins to produce leather which could be used for many purposes. Skins could be impregnated with oils and this early method of tanning, known as 'chamoising', was well known until recent times. Another method that dates back to prehistoric times is that of 'tawing', when alum and salt were applied to a raw hide. In time this produced a white leather which in the recent past was widely valued for making fashionable gloves. Throughout the Middle Ages and until the eighteenth century the great European centre for leather production was Cordova in Spain, and Cordovan leather was sheepskin tawed with alum and sumac and finished with oils to produce leather of superior quality. The cordwainers of Spain, mainly concerned with producing footwear, were famous as craftsmen.

By far the most common method of tanning in post-medieval times was vegetable tanning, where animal pelts were preserved by impregnating skins with tannin. Tannin is present in a wide range of vegetable matter, but the most common source of the chemical was oak bark, obtained preferably from twenty-five or thirty year old coppice oak. This was ground in a bark mill, and mixed with cold water to produce the tanning liquor. Oak-bark tanneries may

be seen at Grampound in Cornwall and Colyton, Devon, and a country tannery from the Mid-Wales town of Rhaeadr has been preserved at the Welsh Folk Museum, St Fagans.

Tanning is a chemical process concerned with the conversion of the gelatinous part of the skin, known as the 'dermis' or 'corium', into leather, by impregnating it with tannic acid. In the tanning process it is the central layer of fibres in a skin which has to be preserved, for the layer above it, the 'epidermis', with the hair or wool growing from it, has to be removed, as has the layer of tissue, fat and flesh below the corium. Both these processes of unhairing and fleshing were carried out by craftsmen known as 'beamsmen', who with a series of knives worked at an upright metal beam in the tannery.

Before the hides were taken to the beam shed, however, they were placed in one of the lime pits in order to loosen the epidermis and the fats and flesh which adhered to the corium or true skin. Slaked lime was mixed with water in varied proportions and placed in the pits. The first pit, in which hides were soaked for a day or two, contained a weak mixture of lime, very often a weak solution of old lime, highly charged with bacteria. The second pit contained a less mellow but a slightly stronger mixture while the third contained a strong solution of new lime. The hides

Tannery workers at Dolgellau, Gwynedd, *c.* 1910

remained in the pits until the hair was easily removed, but the length of liming depended partly on the quality of leather required; the softer the leather, the longer the hide remained in the pit and the mellower the solution. For example, hides designed for sole leather had to be hard and tough, and eight to ten days in a strong lime were sufficient. Harness leather on the other hand, which had to be much more pliable, required mellow liming of twelve to fourteen days, while soft shoe upper leather required anything up to six weeks in weak, mellow lime. The skins were

either suspended by chains from the iron bars at the side of the pits or were allowed to float in the lime solution.

The beamsman then took the blunt-bladed unhairing knife, curved to fit the convex surface of the beam. The hair was easily removed by pressing the hide downwards against the hides. It was important not only to remove the hair but also most of the hair-root sheaths, which could discolour the finished leather. The hair was not thrown away but was sold to plasterers and stone masons as an essential constituent

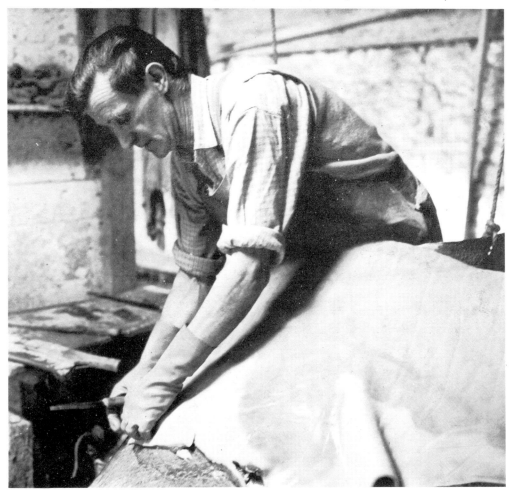

of mortar. Some also went to upholsterers and to manufacturers of cheap clothing.

The fleshing operation was much more skilled than that of unhairing, for the flesh had to be removed in such a way as not to damage the true skin at all. The slightest deviation of the knife would make a hide completely useless. The flesh was shaved away with a very sharp double-edged, two-handled knife. The concave edge was used for scraping, while the convex was for cutting. Fleshings and other matters cut away at this stage were thrown into another pit. The fleshings were then taken away for making glue and gelatine.

To make tanning liquor, the craftsman needed a vast quantity of oak bark, ground finely and mixed with cold water in the so-called 'leaching pits'.

One of the most unpopular tasks at the tannery was that of grinding oak bark, for the fine dust emanating from the water-driven bark mill penetrated everywhere. The large, dried plates of oak bark were taken to the loft above the mill and fed into the hopper of the grinder.

The ground bark was carried from the mill in large baskets to the leading pits where the tanning liquor was made by adding cold water to the bark, and allowing the mixture to stand for some weeks before use. The tanning liquor in various strengths was then pumped to the tan pits proper.

The method of tanning in the old country tanneries consisted of the progression of butts through a series of anything up to fifty tan pits containing liquors of various strengths. The butts were first placed in the suspender pits, a series of eight or ten pits containing the weakest liquors in the tanyard. Each hide was tied to a string and attached to sticks laid across the top of the pit, while a more modern method was to tie the hides to a wooden framework or roller which could be moved gently to and fro to ensure an even

flow of tanning liquids. The hides were moved daily from one pit to the other, the liquors becoming progressively stronger. The tanner had to be very careful the hides did not touch one another in the suspender pits as they would display touch marks and be of uneven colour.

At the end of the suspender stage, the butts with all traces of lime removed would be soft and porous, and they had to be laid flat to straighten out lumps and creases, before being placed in the next set of pits—the handlers or floaters. Here the hides were laid flat rather than suspended and were moved from one pit to the other at regular intervals of two or three days. Tanneries had twelve or more of these handlers, and each one contained continuously stronger liquors. A bucketful of finely ground bark was often

Lime pits at the Rhaeadr Tannery (*Welsh Folk Museum*)

added to the liquor in these pits so as to increase its strength. A long-handled wooden plunger was used to distribute the bark dust evenly throughout the pit, while the spent liquors were pumped back to the suspenders. In the handling pits the hides were moved from one to the other either by means of long-handled tongs or steel hooks.

After some weeks of moving through the series of handlers, the hides then passed to the final set of pits, the layers, which contained the strongest liquors in the yard. Each hide was in this case sprinkled with finely ground oak bark so that each one was saturated with tannin as it sank to the bottom of the pit. Occasionally the liquor in the layer was pumped off, and the partially exhausted vegetable matter removed for further extraction. The hides were then returned to a new liquor until they could absorb no more tannin, a process that took anything up to six weeks.

After the last layer, the fully tanned hides were washed in a weaker solution before being sent to the drying sheds. Before drying, the hides were very lightly oiled with crude cod-liver oil and allowed to dry slowly and evenly. When half dry, they were laid out in a pile with sacks in between each hide and then pinned with the striking pin. This is a triangular-bladed, two-handled knife designed to remove all irregular marks from the hide. Once again the hides were dried, and in order to knit the fibres together, they were placed over a heavy roller. They were usually rolled three times, with a period of drying between each rolling. The whole process of finishing took at least a fortnight and the craftsman had to take great care with the temperature of the drying sheds.

The tanning of leather was a highly complex chemical process and it is surprising how much of these complexities our forefathers knew. A piece of skin would remain in the tanyard for eighteen months and more before it was converted into leather.

Curriers

While the tanner's craft was one which demanded

considerable knowledge of chemical processes, that of the currier demanded a high degree of skill in the use of hand tools that are entirely different from those used by any other leather worker. Currying is to a large extent a mechanical operation: cleansing, reducing in thickness and softening the leather, and impregnating it with oils and fats. The tanner could not complete his work of producing supple leather of good appearance, without the assistance of the currier, for although the finishing employed by the tanner may be good enough for hard, stiff sole leather, it is certainly not good enough for harness and shoe upper leather, where good appearance and suppleness are important.

Although after about 1860 both tanning and currying were more often than not carried out on the same premises, that was not always the case, for it was formerly illegal to carry on together the two trades of tanning and currying; and thus two operations, which were naturally part of the same process, became separated, and leather was dried out by the tanner to be wetted again by the currier, instead of proceeding at once to curry the wet leather.

Currying is a lengthy, complex process and the methods of working depend very largely on the type of leather that is required. The currier has to produce leathers of different weights, grades, colours and supplenesses, by the use of a variety of oils and greases, and the use of a wide range of hand tools.

After delivery from the tanners, the currier's first task was to prepare the leather for dyeing or polishing, by removing the 'bloom' and the dried tanning liquor that clogged up the grain. The hide was soaked and softened in water or in a hot sumac bath. It was then laid on a stone scouring table. Slate tables have a slight inclination so that the hot water, brushed on in ample quantities with a hard brush, ran off. To scrape the bloom from leather, a variety of wooden-handled slickers or stretching irons were used. A slicker has a flat steel blade measuring six inches wide and four inches deep set in a wooden handle. In some

Drying hides (*Welsh Folk Museum*)

cases, copper- or stone-bladed slickers were preferred, but they were not sharpened in any way as this could damage the delicate surface of the leather. For horse hides and other light-coloured leathers, copper slickers were always used, as iron or steel blades could easily blemish the surface of the white leather.

After scouring and slicking, the hides were partially dried or 'sammed' and then shaved or split. The shaving of hides was the most complex of all processes in leather production and it demanded considerable dexterity. The operation was carried out on a wooden beam. The beam consists of a stout square of wood in which the currier stood, and into one end of this a strong hardwood plank was fixed at an angle of eighty degrees. The working surface is formed by a very smooth piece of lignum vitae attached to the upright. Beams varied in size according to the height and preferences of the currier and it was customary for each currier to have his own beam, specially constructed and adjusted to suit him.

The currier's knife is a heavy rectangular, double-edged tool made of fine steel, held by a bar down the centre, with a handle at each end. One handle is horizontal and the other, usually held in the currier's left hand, is vertical. In the early nineteenth century, Cirencester was the centre for the manufacture of these peculiarly shaped knives. Sharpening a currier's knife demanded great skill, for first of all it had to be sharpened with a rubstone and this was followed by rubbing with the cleaning stone, until all the scratches of the rubstone disappeared. The knife was then placed between the craftsman's knees with the straight handle and one end of the cross handle resting on the ground. The edge was then gradually turned over at right angles to the blade by rubbing with a smooth steel held in both hands. The knife had to be resharpened constantly, using a small, wooden-handled steel, almost like a knitting needle, which was passed over the edge, first outside and then down the angle formed by turning.

The process of shaving and skiving was carried out on the flesh side of the hide, and this operation required considerable skill and precision to prevent the knife from cutting too deeply into the surface of the leather.

Certain kinds of leather were subjected to the process of stoning before they were flattened, the craftsman using a stone-bladed slicker or stockstone passed over the grain side of the leather for this process. In this process the grain was smoothed and the leather stretched.

The slicker or stretching iron used at this stage of the work is a plate of iron or steel, set in a wooden handle and sharpened with a rubstone. The scraping beam has a turned edge and in operation skins were placed in water and then laid flat on the table, grain side downward, and the flesh side rubbed with the slicker. Usually two men working from either side of the skin were engaged in slicking, scraping away particles of leather. The grain adhered firmly to the surface of the table and a hard brush with a plentiful supply of water was used for cleaning away the scraped leather. The bloom on the surface of the leather, which had the appearance of a white film, was removed with stockstone and scouring brush, pumice stone and glass slicker, after which the leather was oiled and placed in the drying loft to harden.

The next stage in the processing of leather consisted of brushing its surface with dubbing, a process known as 'stuffing'. The dubbing used at the Rhaeadr tannery was made of equal quantities of tallow and cod oil, the tallow coming from Welsh mountain sheep, whose grease was regarded as far more suitable for making dubbing than that obtained from lowland sheep. The cod oil was usually imported in large casks from Newfoundland. Occasionally, 'sod oil', a greasy substitute obtained in the treatment of sheepskins, was added to the dubbing. At the stuffing stage, the hides had to be slightly moist and the dubbing could be applied to one or both surfaces of the leather. A hard, round brush was used for applying

Currier at work at the Colyton Tannery, Devon, 1974 (*Welsh Folk Museum*)

a thick coat of the oil and the hides were then allowed to dry slowly for some weeks. As the water in the hide evaporated, its place was taken by the liquid part of the dubbing, becoming thoroughly distributed over its surface. The harder fat, known as 'table grease', was left on the surface of the leather and it was afterwards removed by slicking. In a modern tannery, stuffing is completed in a revolving drum.

The surplus grease on the surface of the leather had to be removed after drying with a 'whitening slicker'. Whitening was performed on a sheet of framed plate glass three feet long by two feet wide. This and the whitening slicker, like the currier's knife, has a turned edge that constantly needed turning with the steel. Usually, only the flesh side of a hide was whitened, but occasionally a thin film of the grain, if it was marked in any way, had to be slicked. This particular process was known as 'buffing'. The finishing processes differed considerably according to the type of leather produced. For some leathers a grained effect was required, and this was obtained by rubbing a cork board, usually a convex-soled tool nine inches long and four inches wide attached to the worker's forearm by a leather strap. First the leather was boarded lengthways, then across and finally from corner to corner, so that a pebbled grain of no definite

form resulted. This process also softened the leather.

In some cases the flesh side of a hide had to be blackened and a mixture of lamp black and soap was applied to it. This was followed by a solution of size, prepared by boiling glue in water which, after drying, was smoothed and brightened by glassing or rubbing with a thick, smooth glass slicker. When leather had to be blacked on the grain side, for example harness leather, a mixture of ferrous sulphate and logwood was brushed on it. The leather had to be prepared first by brushing it over with urine or a solution of soda in water. After applying the dyeing solution, the skin was placed grain side on the table and the flesh side shaved with a sharp slicker. It was then turned over again and rubbed with tallow, and finally rubbed with a blunt steel slicker, mahogany board and, according to experienced curriers, with the bare forearm, which gave the black leather a sheen.

In finishing calf leather, widely used for making shoe uppers, the grain side was oiled before stuffing and the flesh side was slicked. Cork was required for raising the grain very slightly, and after gentle slicking of both the flesh and grain side, lamp black was applied to the flesh side. This surface was then glassed a number of times before the skin was cut up ready for use.

The following is a selected list of museums which exhibit craft material. In some cases the more important collections are named. Some of the museums employ working craftsmen, others hold periodic demonstrations by visiting craftsmen.

ABERGAVENNY (Gwent): Saddler's shop and a small collection of local craft material.

ALTON (Hants): Extensive collections of craft tools from north Hampshire, including rake, besom and hurdle making.

ASTON MUNSLOW (Salop): Cider making, carts and wagons.

AYLESBURY (Bucks): Rural Life Gallery.

BAKEWELL (Derbys.)

BASINGSTOKE (Hants): Clock- and watch-making material.

BATH—American Museum: North American crafts.

BEAMISH (Durham): A large and comprehensive collection of craft and industrial material relating to the North of England. Craft demonstrations by full-time and visiting craftsmen.

BEWDLEY (Heref. and Worcs.): Excellent collection of crafts relating to the Wyre Forest, including charcoal burning, coopering and spale-basket making. Demonstrations by visiting craftsmen.

BICTON, EAST BUDLEIGH (Devon): Cider, wagons.

BIRMINGHAM—Sarehole Mill: Corn and grinding mill.

BLACKBURN—Lewis Textile Museum.

BOLTON—Tonge Hall Textile Machinery Museum.

BRADFORD—Industrial Museum.

BRIDPORT (Dorset): Nets and rope-making equipment.

BRISTOL—Blaise Castle House Museum: Corn Mill, craft tools.

BROMSGROVE—Avoncraft Museum of Buildings.

BURNLEY—Towneley Hall Museum: Local craft material.

CALDERDALE (West Yorks.)—Shibden Hall, Halifax: Reconstructed craft workshops.

CAMBRIDGE—Folk Museum: Extensive collection of Fenland crafts.

CHICHESTER (West Sussex)—Weald and Downland Open-Air Museum: Charcoal burning clamp and re-erected buildings.

COLCHESTER.

CREGNEACH (Isle of Man): Weaver's shop, turner's cottage and smithy in a village setting.

DONCASTER (South Yorks.)—Cusworth Hall Museum.

DORCHESTER.

DUDLEY—Black Country Museum.

111

EXETER—Maritime Museum.

FILKINS (Glos.)—Cotswold Craft Museum.

GLOUCESTER—Bishop Hooper's Lodging: Fishery crafts are especially important.

HARTLEBURY (Heref. and Worcs.): Extensive collection of craft material including restored cider mill.
HEREFORD.
HIGH WYCOMBE (Bucks.)—Wycombe Chair and Local History Museum.
HORSHAM (West Sussex): Smithy, wheelwright and saddler's shop, wagons.
HUTTON-LE-HOLE (North Yorks.)—Ryedale Folk Museum: Extensive collection including smithy and glass furnace.

KEIGHLEY (West Yorks.).
KENDAL—Abbot Hall Museum of Lakeland Life and Industry.
KINGSBRIDGE (Devon)—Cookworthy Museum.
KING'S LYNN (Norfolk).

LEEDS—Abbey House Museum: Reconstructed workshops.
LEICESTER—Newarke Houses Museum.
LINCOLN—Museum of Lincolnshire Life.
LLANBERIS (Gwynedd)—North Wales Quarrying Museum.
LLANVAPLEY (Gwent)—Rural Crafts Museum.
LOOE—The Cornish Museum.
LUDLOW (Salop).
LUTON: Straw hat and lace making in particular.

MAIDSTONE (Kent)—Tyrwhitt-Drake Museum of Carriages.

NEWPORT (Gwent).
NORTHAMPTON—Museum of Leather: Footwear especially.

NORWICH—Bridewell Museum of Local Industries and Rural Crafts.

OAKHAM (Leics.)—Rutland County Museum.

READING—Museum of English Rural Life: A national collection of craft equipment and documentary material. Carts and wagons.

ST ALBANS—City Museum: Includes the unique Salaman collection of craft tools.
ST FAGANS (South Glamorgan)—Welsh Folk Museum: An extensive collection of craft material from Wales. The Museum employs a full-time blacksmith, two weavers, two wood turners and a cooper. There is also a re-erected tannery, corn mill and woollen mill, together with a branch museum, the Museum of the Woollen Industry at Dre-fach Felindre, Dyfed.
SCUNTHORPE.
SHEFFIELD—Abbeydale Industrial Hamlet: Preserved scythe-works.
SHUGBOROUGH—Staffordshire County Museum.
STOKE-ON-TRENT—Gladstone Pottery Museum.
STOWMARKET (Suffolk)—Abbot's Hall Museum of Rural Life of East Anglia: Re-erected smithy with working blacksmith, water mill and an extensive collection of craft material.
STROUD.

TELFORD (Salop)—Ironbridge Gorge Museum.

WALSALL (West Midlands).
WARWICK.
WEYBRIDGE (Surrey).
WISBECH (Cambs.).
WOODSTOCK—Oxfordshire County Museum.

YORK—Castle Museum: Extensive collection including re-erected corn mill.

rope maker's stall in Carmarthen market, *c.* 1930 (*M. L. Wight*)

BOOKS FOR FURTHER READING

ALEXANDER, Bruce (ed.), *Crafts and Craftsmen* (Croom Helm, 1974).

ARNOLD, James, *The Countryman's Workshop* (Phoenix House, 1953).

ARNOLD, James, *The Shell Book of Country Crafts* (John Baker, 1968).

BLANDFORD, Percy W., *Country Craft Tools* (David & Charles, 1974).

CLIFTON-TAYLOR, A., *The Pattern of English Building* (Faber, 1972).

EDLIN, H.L., *Woodland Crafts in Britain* (Batsford, 1949).

EDWARDS, E.H., *Saddlery* (J. A. Allen, 1971).

HUGHES, G. Bernard, *Living Crafts* (Lutterworth Press, 1953).

IRESON, Barbara, *Cottage Crafts* (Faber, 1975).

JENKINS, J.G., *The Craft Industries* (Longmans, 1972).

JENKINS, J.G., *The English Farm Wagon* (David & Charles, 1972).

JENKINS, J.G., *Nets and Coracles* (David & Charles, 1974).

JENKINS, J.G., *Traditional Country Craftsmen* (Routledge, 1965).

JENKINS, J.G., (ed.), *The Wool Textile Industry in Great Britain* (Routledge, 1972).

JONES, J.L., *Crafts and the Countryside* (David & Charles, 1975).

KILBY, K., *The Cooper and his Trade* (John Baker, 1971).

MANNERS, J.E., *Country Crafts Today* (David & Charles, 1974).

MAYES, L.J., *A History of Chair Making in High Wycombe* (Routledge, 1960).

NIALL, I., *The Country Blacksmith* (Heinemann, 1966).

OXFORD UNIVERSITY, Agricultural Economics Research Institute, *The Rural Industries of England and Wales*, 4 vols. (O.U.P., 1926–7).

PEATE, I.C., *Welsh Folk Crafts and Industries* (National Museum of Wales, 1935).

WATERER, J.W., *Leather Craftsmanship* (Faber, 1956).

WEBBER, R., *The Village Blacksmith* (David & Charles, 1971).

WOODS, K.S., *Rural Crafts of England* (EP Publishing Ltd, 1975).

WYMER, N., *English Country Crafts* (Batsford, 1946).

WYMER, N., *English Town Crafts* (Batsford, 1949).